P9-DFR-465

A BUSINESS
SUCCESS GUIDE

Speed Reading

By

Steve Moidel
President
Allstate Speed Reading Center
Westlake Village, CA

BARRON'S

Dedicated with love to my wife, Gayle, and my son, Matthew.

All inquiries should be addressed to:
Barron's Educational Series, Inc.
250 Wireless Boulevard
Hauppauge, New York 11788

Library of Congress Catalog Card No. 94-25370

International Standard Book No. 0-8120-1845-1

Library of Congress Cataloging-in-Publication Data

Moidel, Steve.
    Speed reading / Steve Moidel.
        p.   cm.
    "Barron's a business success guide."
    Includes index.
    ISBN 0-8120-1845-1
    1. Rapid reading. I. Title.
LB1050.54.M65   1994
428.4'3—dc20   94-25370
                                                            CIP

PRINTED IN THE UNITED STATES OF AMERICA
4567   9770   987654321

CONTENTS

CHAPTER 1 SPEED READING: GETTING STARTED

Questions to keep in mind: What is effective speed reading? How much of an increase in reading speed can you expect? How much time will you have to invest? Is speed reading a necessary skill?

WHY SPEED READING?

In today's high-tech world, the printed word is bombarding you at an unparalleled pace. A deluge of material flows daily from computers, fax machines, cellular phones, cable, not to mention conventional newspapers, magazines, technical journals, mail, and, yes, even books. Recently the Xerox Corporation estimated that the average business executive must read over a million words per week just to keep current. So what high-tech tool do you have to help you absorb and assimilate this flood of information? The answer is "none." With all our modern technological wizardry, you are still reading at the same rate of speed as your great-grandparents did over a hundred years ago.

But that will soon change. Your reading skills are about to be upgraded and redesigned for learning in the twenty-first century. Effective speed reading will supercharge your learning ability for today and tomorrow's *information superhighway* by teaching you how to maximize your brain's potential.

WHO NEEDS SPEED READING?

The ability to speed read is essential for any person who wants to keep up with our rapidly changing world. One could even argue that effective speed reading should be a prerequisite for all of the business and financial communities, professional people in all fields, and students from junior high on. But it isn't. The reality is that most people will never make any effort to improve their reading and learning skills. The fact that you are reading this now puts you in a select minority. Do not take this lightly. Effective speed reading gives you a competitive edge that can propel you to the top of your profession.

Francis Bacon wrote that "knowledge is power." If this statement is true, then the knowledge that gives you the most power is how to obtain the most knowledge. Effective speed reading brings you to the threshold of this great power.

WHAT IS EFFECTIVE SPEED READING?

Effective speed reading is not just reading faster, it's reading smarter. It combines the interrelated skills of concentration, comprehension, and recall with speed reading. You'll learn how to be a flexible reader and how to master even the most difficult or technical material quickly and easily.

IS SPEED READING EASY?

Speed reading is a psychomotor skill. It is no more difficult to learn than playing tennis, typing, or sewing. Almost anyone who is motivated and can read on a fourth-grade level can learn the skill of speed reading.

HOW FAST CAN I LEARN TO SPEED READ?

You can learn the basics of speed reading in an hour or two. In that short amount of time, you can double your reading speed with as good or better comprehension. However, that doesn't mean you will be an expert or an advanced speed reader. No one becomes an expert in anything in just a few hours. To become an advanced speed reader, a certain amount of dedication and practice is required. A minimum investment of 45 minutes to an hour each day for the next six weeks can transform speed reading into a lifetime skill. This small investment will pay you large dividends for the rest of your learning life. For maximum benefit you may choose to use business-related material for your practice.

MATERIALS YOU WILL NEED

You will need the following materials for each session: a book of your choice (it should be at least 250 pages long), a desk or a table on which to position the book, two paper clips, a notebook, a pencil or a pen, and a timing device such as a clock or stopwatch. Take the time to gather these items now.

HOW TO MEASURE PROGRESS

To measure progress, choose for your practice a book that doesn't have many illustrations, photos, and other visual material. After each reading, estimate your comprehension and then decide your reading rate. A more detailed explanation on how to estimate comprehension and compute reading rates follows. If you prefer a more formal way to measure progress, you may consider purchasing a test preparatory book (Barron's SAT, LSAT, GRE, etc.) that includes timed reading comprehension sections. Also, Chapter 12 includes a timed reading for both speed and comprehension.

HOW TO DETERMINE READING RATES
IN YOUR OWN MATERIAL

To determine reading rates in your own material follow this procedure:

1. Place a paper clip at your beginning spot.
2. You will need an accurate way to time yourself. Use a clock, stopwatch, or any other timing device. Be sure to write down the exact time you start if you are using a standard watch or clock.
3. When you complete the reading, immediately record your ending time and determine the total time you spent reading, estimated to the nearest quarter minute. For example, if you read for 4 minutes and 56 seconds, round it off to 5 minutes; if it was 5 minutes and 27 seconds, round it off to 5.5 minutes.
4. Count the number of words in four full lines and divide the number by four. This will give you your average words per line (a.w.p.l.).
Example: 40 words in 4 full lines divided by 4 = 10 a.w.p.l.
5. Count the number of lines on one complete page and multiply that total by your average words per line. This gives you your average words per page (a.w.p.p.).
Example: 38 lines on a complete page × 10 a.w.p.l. = 380 a.w.p.p.
6. Count the number of complete pages that you read (do not count a partial page) and multiply that number by the average words per page.
Example: 5 complete pages × 380 a.w.p.p. = 1900 words
7. Count the number of lines you read on any partial page and multiply that figure by your average words per line.
Example: 5 lines on a partial page × 10 = 50 words

8. Add Steps 6 and 7 and then divide that total by your reading time. This gives you your average words per minute (a.w.p.m.) during that reading session.

Example: 1900 + 50 = 1950 total words

$$\frac{1950 \text{ (total words)}}{5 \text{ minutes}} = 390 \text{ a.w.p.m.}$$

HOW TO ESTIMATE COMPREHENSION

Throughout this book, you will be asked to do many readings. Often they will be only one minute in length. Estimate your comprehension in the following way:

1. Ask yourself how much of the material you comprehended. Comprehension does not mean that you can recall all the information. Comprehension and recall are two separate skills. How much of the material did you understand at the moment you were reading it?

2. Estimate a number percentage based on this criteria. In nonfiction material, for you to have 50 percent comprehension means that you understand the main ideas with little or no details; with 60 percent comprehension you understand the main points and attach some details, and with 80 percent comprehension you understand the main ideas and can connect most of the details.

HOW FAST DO YOU READ?

Do you know how fast you are presently reading? Chances are you don't. Most people put themselves in general reading speed categories, such as "I'm a slow reader." However, to gauge progress, you need first to determine your present reading speed.

1. In practice material of your choice, place a paper clip on the line where you will begin reading.

2. Time yourself and read for one minute for your best comprehension. Read normally or comfortably. Place a clip on the line where you stop.

3. Estimate your comprehension as described previously.

4. Determine your reading rate for that one minute. Record your beginning reading rate and estimated comprehension on the first line of the Daily Progress Report Sheet that can be found in the back of this book.

Now that you know your present reading speed, you need to decide exactly what you want out of this book. How fast do you want to read? What is realistic? Can you improve comprehension along with speed? The answers to these questions, and many more, are coming up next.

CHAPTER 2 ATTITUDE, GOALS, AND SPEED READING

*Questions to keep in mind: Goals need
to contain what two elements to be
effective? What are the main
differences between the right and left
hemispheres of your brain? How do
you control frustration?*

Your success as a speed reader will have more to do
with your mind-set than with your present reading
speed or any innate ability that you presently possess. Attitude is as important in speed reading as in any
sport or game. There are three main factors in developing the proper attitude for maximum results.

1. SET GOALS

To a certain degree you are already goal oriented, otherwise you would not be reading this book. Nonetheless, every exercise and reading from this point on will
have a clearly defined purpose. In order for your goals
to be effective they must be both *realistic* and *specific*.

Realistic Short-term Goals

All long-term goals should be broken into smaller, more
manageable parts. For example, if you are presently
reading 200 w.p.m. and your long-term goal is to read
1000 w.p.m., the discrepancy is so great that you may
become discouraged and give up before you reach
your goal. On the other hand, if you work in short-term

increments of 50 to 100 w.p.m., your first subgoal might be to read 300 w.p.m. This subgoal is realistic and accessible. When you reach 300 w.p.m., you reset your short-term goal to 400 w.p.m. and so on, until you ultimately reach your 1000 w.p.m. long-term goal.

Specific Goals

Notice that in the preceding example the goals are extremely specific: the long-term goal is 1000 w.p.m. and the first subgoal is 300 w.p.m. It is not nearly as effective to say "I want to read faster" or "I want good comprehension." These statements are far too general. Your mind needs a specific target to focus on in order to create and implement the appropriate plan of action. Once your mind knows exactly what you want, it automatically begins to work toward the realization of your goal, and your chances for success are greatly enhanced.

2. ACT AS IF YOUR GOAL HAS ALREADY BEEN ACCOMPLISHED

Accept as fact, right from the beginning, that reaching your speed reading goal is inevitable. You will succeed. No *and*'s, *if*'s, or *but*'s. You can compare learning these speed reading methods to going on a summer vacation. This book is your road map. If you follow the map and the directions are good (and they will be), you will reach your final destination.

There are two distinct ways to act as if your goal has already been accomplished, and they deal with the inherent differences between the right and left hemispheres of your brain. This distinction between the two sides of your brain will not only be applicable for this session on goal setting, but will be a major principle in helping you master the speed reading, memory, and concentration techniques coming up in subsequent chapters.

Right Brain–Left Brain

Recent brain research suggests that the right and left hemispheres of your brain are responsible for different aspects of human behavior and performance. The left hemisphere of your brain deals with the more analytical or logical areas such as math, science, organizational skills, and language. The right side of your brain deals predominantly with the more creative areas such as art, music, humor, and visual imagery. For our purposes in this section on goal setting, let's simplify the distinction between the two by stating that the right hemisphere is visual whereas the left hemisphere is verbal.

The majority of people who set goals do so by either stating or writing verbal affirmations. For example, if you want to lose weight, you might say to yourself, "I want to lose ten pounds by Thanksgiving." When you verbalize your goals, what part of your brain have you activated? Your left hemisphere, because you are dealing with language. But have you done anything to involve the right part of your brain? No, and unless you actively involve both sides of your brain, you may encounter a *canceling out effect*. For instance, you may write down and mentally repeat to yourself that you are reading 1000 words per minute with 85 percent comprehension, but your right brain may conjure up images of you reading slowly, and thus the right and left parts of your brain will cancel out one another. Conversely, you may visualize yourself as a super speed reader with excellent comprehension; yet, your inner voice repeats such statements as *"Who are you trying to fool? You know that you can't read that fast."* Once again, the right and left hemispheres of your brain are in conflict and cancel out one another.

The key is to have both sides of your brain working in harmony to accomplish a common goal. So not only must you *tell* yourself that you are reading at 1000 w.p.m. with 85 percent comprehension (left brain), you must *visualize* yourself reading that fast (right brain). This whole-brain approach to goal setting is powerful and effective.

3. LET NO ONE DISCOURAGE YOU

Once you set a goal and act as if that goal has already been accomplished, you must let absolutely no one discourage you from reaching it. You must close your mind to critics. Have you ever noticed how people want to tell you why you can't do something, why it's impossible? You often hear these types of things from co-workers, friends, and even relatives. They seem to want you to fail. But why? The unfortunate truth is that some people like to keep other people at a level of inadequacy similar to their own. Another way of saying this is: *Misery loves company.* If you tell someone: "I'm going to read three times faster," he may point out every reason you can't. The bottom line is that it takes little effort to be a critic and stifle someone else's ambition. What isn't so easy is to invest the time, money, and effort it takes to better yourself. Close your ears to negative outside voices and focus on your goal.

However, discouragement does not always come from outer critics. It also comes from within. It is the paradox of human nature that often we become our own worst enemy. In learning the skill of speed reading, you will most definitely encounter frustration. There is always a certain amount of frustration in learning anything new. The key is to not allow the frustration to rage out of control. So how do you control frustration? Relax.

Effective speed reading is a mental discipline. All true mind disciplines, whether the martial arts, meditation, or yoga, start with the art of relaxation. Speed reading is no exception. Throughout the book you will learn various relaxation techniques. However, one of the easiest and fastest ways to relax is through the use of proper breathing techniques as described in the following exercise.

Diaphragm Deep-Breathing Exercise

1. Sit comfortably with your arms at your sides.
2. Using your diaphragm (in your stomach region), take a deep, slow breath through your nose for a count of four.
3. Hold your breath for a count of four.
4. Still using your diaphragm, exhale through your mouth for a count of four.
5. Rest for a count of four.
6. Repeat six to ten times or until relaxed.

Make it a habit to use this simple deep-breathing exercise anytime you feel the need to relax. This will also help you cope with the normal stresses of your work day.

YOUR SPEED READING GOALS

On the next page you will find two speed reading goal statements, one for your long-term reading goal and one for your realistic short-term goal. The next section will help you determine the numbers to fill in the blanks. Notice that there is no hint of doubt in these goal statements, such as "I *hope to be* reading, I *should be* reading, I *want to be* reading." The goals are stated in the present tense, in a positive direct way.

Furthermore, don't just fill in the blanks. Your goals will be more effective if you rewrite each statement in your own handwriting. This will help you to accept and internalize these goal statements as your own and to crystallize them in your mind.

Long-term

I am reading _____ words per minute with ____% comprehension.

Short-term

I am reading _____ words per minute with ____% comprehension.

WHAT IS REALISTIC?

Now it's time to fill in the blanks with realistic numbers. The numbers are based on your own personal needs. How fast do you want to read? How much time and effort are you willing or able to invest in speed reading skills? How much reading will you have to do?

If you can invest an hour a day for the next six weeks, it is realistic to expect a three- to five-time increase in your reading speed and a 5 to 10 percent increase in comprehension. Even with only a few hours of practice, you can *double* your present reading speed either at your same level of comprehension or with slightly better understanding of the material.

Let's assume you can practice an hour a day for six weeks, and you are presently reading 200 w.p.m. with 70 percent comprehension. You may set your long-term speed reading goal at 1000 w.p.m. with 80 percent comprehension. To reach your long-term goal, you must first set short-term goals that are realistic and accessible. For example, your first subgoal might be to read 300 w.p.m. with 71 percent comprehension. When you reach that subgoal, you'd reset it to 400 w.p.m. with 72 percent comprehension, and so on until you reach your long-term goal.

THE GOAL-SETTING PROCESS

Have your short- and long-term speed reading goals in
front of you and follow this procedure:

1. Relax using the deep-breathing exercise. Inhale
   through your nose for a count of four using your diaphragm, hold for a count of four, exhale through the
   mouth for a count of four, rest for a count of four. Repeat until you begin to feel relaxed.
2. Now read your realistic and specific long-term and
   short-term goal statements (left brain) while visualizing the benefits (right brain). Conjure up the feelings
   and emotions that you will feel reading so much faster
   with excellent concentration, comprehension, and recall; think about what you can accomplish by being a
   super speed reader.

   If you have followed these instructions, you have
just seen your final destination. Now, let's begin to turn
those words and pictures into reality.

CHAPTER 3

THE SIX MAJOR READING PROBLEMS

Questions to keep in mind: Are you presently a slow, average, or fast reader? What do speed readers do or not do that allows them to read so much more effectively than average readers? What factors presently inhibit your reading speed and comprehension?

The average reading speed in the United States is 252 words per minute. However, if you're reading between 150 and 350 words per minute, you are an average or normal reader. Chances are that your own reading speed falls within this range. What then separates you from the person who can read 500 to 1000 words per minute or faster? The answer lies in six common reading problems that speed readers have learned to overcome. Let's cover each of these problems in detail.

1. WORD-BY-WORD READING

One of the main differences between the average reader and a speed reader is the way you presently look at the page. Open your book to any full page of print and focus on it as if you were getting ready to read. What exactly are you seeing? Most likely your eyes fixate on one line, or perhaps one or two words within that line. Now turn the book upside down, so that the print is upside down, and look at that same page again. Do you notice a difference in your focus? Chances are, you can easily see larger areas of the page, maybe whole paragraphs as if they were blocks of print, or perhaps even the whole page, as an abstract painting or design.

Now, turn your book right side up and watch what happens to your eyes. Most likely you are noticing another switch in focus. As soon as your eyes recognize some of the words, they zoom in on just one or two words in an individual line. This change occurs because of the way you were conditioned to read from the earliest age.

Starting in the first grade, you read one word at a time, moving across an individual line. When you finished one line, you began the very next line and most likely you've been reading this way ever since. Speed readers, on the other hand, see and read groups of words at a time. This method is not only much faster, but also improves concentration and comprehension for reasons that will be discussed shortly.

2. LACK OF CONCENTRATION

Does this sound familiar? You read a page—it could be in a business journal, textbook, novel, or other material—and when you reach the bottom of the page you think, "I don't know what I just read." You then must backtrack and read the same material again, and if it's an exceptionally bad day, perhaps even a third time. This is a problem in concentration, which of course affects your comprehension. No matter how intelligent you are, you can't comprehend what you never had your mind on to begin with.

On the surface of this problem, it's interesting to think about where your mind goes when it isn't on that page. Sometimes your mind is in the next office listening to a discussion, or perhaps you hear voices down the hall or traffic moving outside, or maybe you begin to daydream. For example, you may be reading a paragraph and suddenly you come to a word like *party* and the next thing you know you're thinking about a party you attended which has absolutely nothing to do with what you're reading. Often when you enter one of these daydreaming dazes, you will still go through all the motions of reading. You look at words, you turn pages, and sometimes you may even turn six or seven pages before you realize that none of the information is being absorbed. You have to go back now and reread the material at least one more time.

Why does loss of concentration happen so often especially when you read? To answer this question let's use the analogy of the human brain to the computer. The human brain is the most powerful computer on this planet. The best computer that IBM has can't even come close to duplicating what your brain can do. Yet, when you sit down to read, you feed this supercomputer that you possess one...word...at...a...time.

Reading as you presently experience it is just too slow. You get bored, and your mind wanders off. In fact, have you ever used reading as a sedative before you go to sleep? Perhaps you read a page or two and your eyes start to close. Many people all over the world use reading as a nightly ritual to help themselves fall asleep.

Related to this problem is the fact that your brain is in constant need of stimulation. Your brain will actively search out stimulation elsewhere if you don't give it enough. That's exactly the problem when you read one word at a time. At that speed, you rarely give your brain enough stimulation, so if there happens to be more going on in the next office or even in your own daydreams, that's where your mind goes.

Now, let's look at this problem of concentration from an entirely different perspective. Imagine for just a moment that you could read at 1000 words per minute. Approximately one hundred years ago, William James, the great psychologist, estimated that the average person used less than 10 percent of his or her brain's real potential. However, many experts now believe that this estimate is high and that most people actually use less than 2 percent of their brain's true ability. Nonetheless, even if you accepted the higher figure of 10 percent, that's still just a fraction of the real power of your brain. If you read at 1000 words per minute, you simply utilize more of your brain's potential. In addition, you achieve the purpose of giving your mind enough stimulation. At that speed, your mind would have little desire to go elsewhere. The bottom line is: fill up the mind, and it will wander less.

3. SUBVOCALIZATION–YOUR INNER VOICE

Another reading problem that presently keeps you from reading faster is that little voice you hear inside your head whenever you read. What voice? The voice you are almost certainly hearing at this very moment. You are pronouncing the words silently inside your head as you read.

Subvocalization is the number one problem that presently limits your reading speed. Think about it logically: if you pronounce the words inwardly as you read them, you then limit your reading speed to your speaking speed. Most people can't talk faster than a few hundred words per minute and that's the main reason the average reading speed is 252 words per minute.

In order for you to become a true speed reader, you must learn to reduce the problem of subvocalization. However, before you can reduce your inner voice, it's important to have an understanding of why you subvocalize. Think back to when you were just learning how to read. Do you remember sitting in a reading circle, with a big book in the center, usually with three or four words on a page? You and your classmates would take turns reading aloud. You would hear your teacher's voice, your own voice, and then all of your classmates' voices in succession. Even at home, when your parents or grandparents read you a bedtime story, what choice did they have but to read it aloud? Then there came the day, during the first year of school, when your teacher said, "Class, I want all of you now to read silently to yourselves." At that moment, you internalized that voice and it has most likely been inside your head ever since.

During the first three years of school, subvocalization is absolutely necessary because initially you have to know how to pronounce the words phonetically. However, that is not true once you have a fourth-grade reading proficiency because by that time most of the words in your vocabulary are "sight words." A sight word is a word that is unnecessary to pronounce inwardly to know what it means. You are surrounded by sight words: book, table, pencil, paper, telephone; these are words you've seen countless times. For example, if you look at your hand right now, do you have to say *hand* to know that you're looking at it? Of course not, but when you come across the word *hand* on the page, you still pronounce it inside your head as if you're seeing it for the first time.

But that's not the worst part of the problem. At this moment, can you think of a good definition for the word *the*? Take your time now. Even if you came up with the fact that *the* is a definite article, that still doesn't define what the word means. A word like *the* only has meaning within the context in which it's used. This is true not only of *the*, but also of words such as *a, and, to,* and *of.* These are known as structure words.

Structure words are the glue words to the sentence. They introduce nouns, they connect parts of sentences and phrases, but by themselves they convey very little meaning. In fact, many of these structure words are very similar to punctuation marks. For example, often an *and* and a comma could be interchanged, but there is a major difference between the two. When you are reading and you come to a punctuation mark, do you say to yourself *question mark, exclamation point, quotation marks*? Of course you don't. At this point, you almost certainly recognize punctuation marks on sight, but that is not the case when you come to a structure word. You still pronounce these words as if they were the most important words on the page and as if they were conveying a whole lot of meaning to you.

Here is a statistic that will bring this problem of subvocalization into perspective. There are over one million words in the English language and out of these words there are approximately four hundred structure words. Now, four hundred out of one million is certainly not a large percentage, but those four hundred structure words on the average make up 60 percent of every written page you have ever read or will ever read. That's a lot of *and*'s, *the*'s, *of*'s, and *to*'s you've been pronouncing inside your head all these years and a lot more you're going to continue to say unless you do something about this problem.

Also, it's important to make the distinction of not subvocalizing words as opposed to skipping words. You will not be taught to skip words in this book. If you missed an *or* or a *but*, you could misconstrue the meaning of the whole sentence or paragraph. However, you will learn to be able to see these words, understand them, but simply not pronounce them inside your head, similar again to the way you can now do this with punctuation marks.

Furthermore, you must accept the fact that you will most likely never completely eliminate the problem of subvocalization nor should you really try. Your objective is to reduce the problem gradually until the only words you still pronounce will be the unfamiliar words and the words that convey the most meaning to you.

4. INADEQUATE VOCABULARY

Having an inadequate vocabulary is a problem that there is no simple solution for. Sometimes when you come to a word you're not familiar with there is no alternative but to look it up in the dictionary. However, the reality is that most people will not take the time to consult a dictionary every time they come to a word they don't know. So how then do you build a powerful vocabulary? First, you must acquire a base knowledge of common root prefixes that appear at the beginning of words, and suffixes that appear at the end of words. In Chapter 11, the most commonly used prefixes and suffixes are included along with an easy system to commit them to memory.

Another method to improve your vocabulary is a bit more unconventional and requires that you utilize the speed reading methods you will be learning shortly. Speed readers are more involved in the thoughts or ideas being presented. Consequently, when a speed reader comes to an isolated word or phrase he doesn't know the meaning of, he is often able to deduce its meaning from the context in which it is being used.

Furthermore, by speed reading, you'll find yourself reading far more material than you do presently. Over time, this exposure to additional words will have a positive effect on your vocabulary without any real conscious effort on your part.

5. UNCONSCIOUS REGRESSION

Unconscious regression occurs when you reread words that you've already read because your eyes make a mistake. For example, you read a line, move your eyes to what you believe to be the next line, but instead end up rereading the line you just finished. A variation of this problem happens when you read a line and think your eyes have moved to the next line, but your eyes have actually jumped down a line or two too far. In both cases, the end result is the same: you must reread material you've already read because your eyes have made a mistake.

The average reader spends approximately one-sixth of his reading time regressing. The reason for this problem is based on a misconception about how the eyes work. Most people assume their eyes work almost like a typewriter return when they read. They picture their eyes moving from line to line quickly and smoothly. Unfortunately, eyes don't work that way. Your eyes move in very jerky starts and stops known as *saccades*. The good news is that the problem of unconscious regression is quite easy to correct, and by the end of the next chapter you'll learn how to practically eliminate it.

6. SLOW RECOVERY TIME

A reading problem related to regression and the way your eyes function is *slow recovery time*. This is a major reading problem that most people are completely unaware of. Recovery time refers to the time that it takes your eyes to move from the end of one line back to begin the very next one.

The average reader spends up to one-third of her reading time just looking for the next line. This means that approximately one hour out of every three hours you read, all you are doing is searching for the next line; there is no information coming in. That's a lot of time looking for *nothing*! In fact, by correcting only the problems of slow recovery time and of unconscious regression, you can double your reading speed—and you'll learn how to do just that in Chapter 4.

Points to Remember

1. The major differences between average readers and speed readers are reflected in six common reading problems: *word-by-word reading, lack of concentration, subvocalization, inadequate vocabulary, unconscious regression,* and *slow recovery time.*

2. A trained speed reader learns to read groups of words at a time. By doing so, he not only reads faster, but improves concentration by utilizing more of his brain's potential.

3. A speed reader limits the number of words she pronounces inwardly, only subvocalizing important or unfamiliar words.
4. A speed reader reads for concepts or ideas, and unfamiliar words are often discerned within the context in which they're used.
5. A speed reader rarely regresses, and moves from line to line quickly and smoothly.

CHAPTER 4

DOUBLE YOUR READING SPEED IN AN HOUR

Questions to keep in mind: Are all speed reading methods the same? What does the hand have to do with speed reading?

Imagine how much more productive you'd be if you doubled your reading speed. What could it mean in terms of your career? What would you do with all that extra free time? These are not just idle questions. An hour from now you could easily be reading twice as fast by using a simple, effective method. Sound interesting? Then fasten your seat belt because reading may never be quite the same again.

A BRIEF HISTORY OF SPEED READING

One of the first of the speed reading disciplines to become popular after World War II used a machine called a tachistoscope. A tachistoscope is a device that controls how long a shutter is open and allows light in for various intervals of time. By using this method, words can be flashed on a screen progressively faster. The objective is to increase reading speed by gradually adjusting a person's vision and reaction time. The tachistoscope method works for some people initially, but the results are usually temporary since you must continually use the machine to maintain speed. Unless you own a tachistoscope, or have access to one on a daily basis, you are likely to regress to your original reading rate.

Another discipline of speed reading that became popular during the late 1940s and early 1950s advocated strictly the use of faster eye movements to increase reading speed. As with the tachistoscope, some people did increase their reading speed initially, but few continued to use the technique long term. The primary flaw with the eye movement technique is that it doesn't take into account the way your eyes work naturally. Your eyes move in very jerky, sporadic motions, not in a straight line. By attempting to retrain the eyes to do something that is not natural, many people found the eye movement technique difficult and extremely frustrating.

VISUAL GUIDES—THE SPEED READING HAND

For approximately ten years, speed reading camps were divided into the machine or eye movement schools, but then a third method combined the best of both schools in a unique way. The method that changed speed reading forever resulted from the discovery of the effectiveness of pacing devices or visual guides for the eyes. Index cards, pens, pencils have all been used, but the most popular and most effective of the pacing devices is the hand. As you will soon discover for yourself, the hand replaces the tachistoscope and becomes your own personal reading machine. Consequently, as long as you have your hand, your reading machine is ready to go. Furthermore, it is a flexible machine. You determine how fast you move it down the page. This gives you complete control. You can speed up in easier, unnecessary, or redundant readings or slow down proportionally in difficult, important, or detailed material. These are only the general advantages of using the hand for speed reading. Following is a brief discussion of some other benefits:

1. Helps You Read Groups of Words. One of the keys to effective speed reading is reading groups of words at a time. The hand helps you to easily section off and then read areas of print by pacing the eyes over the material with an open focus.

2. **Reduces Subvocalization.** The hand helps to reduce subvocalization by pacing the eyes down the page faster than you can pronounce each word. By doing this you must choose which words you continue to say inside of your head. With additional practice, you will learn to subvocalize primarily important or unfamiliar words and less structure and sight words.

3. **Reduces Regression and Slow Recovery Time.** Using the hand dramatically reduces the eye problems of regression and slow recovery time. These two mechanical problems of the eyes account for almost half of your reading time. A more detailed account of how the hand reduces these two problems will be given shortly.

4. **Creates Attention on the Material.** The hand helps to create attention on the material, which is an element of good concentration. When you use your hand as a pacing device, reading is no longer a passive process; you literally become physically involved with the material as you add the sense of touch to reading.

5. **Adds Rhythm.** Reading has a beat when you use your hand as a pacer. With practice, your hand motions will become smooth and rhythmic. Why is this important? Because it brings the right part of your brain into the reading process. Reading is a left brain activity since it deals with language. Music and rhythm are right brain activities. By using your hand as a pacer when you read, you indirectly involve the right side of your brain, resulting in a positive effect on your concentration, comprehension, and recall.

THE SPEED READING QUICK START TECHNIQUE

The first speed reading technique that uses your hand as a pacer is called the Quick Start. This method requires only the use of your index finger. If you're right-handed, you'll use your right index finger; if you're left-handed, you'll use your left. Start by forming your hand in the shape of a fist; then keeping all your other fingers and the thumb tucked underneath, allow only

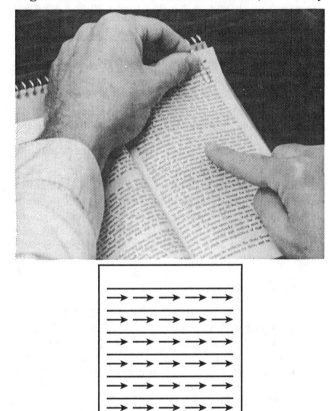

Reading hand motion

Figure 4A
The Speed Reading Quick Start Technique

your index finger to point outward. In your practice book, underline every line from margin to margin using your index finger as if you were underlining the words with a pencil or a pen (see Figure 4A). Focus on the words directly above your fingertip. At this point, do not concern yourself with comprehension. It will take you a few minutes to begin to feel comfortable with the mechanics of the Quick Start underlining technique.

When you finish a line, bring your index finger back to the beginning of the next line with a motion as *fast and smooth* as you can make it. It is important that the return be fluid. If you jerk your finger back, it may become a distraction and ultimately hurt your comprehension. Pretend that your finger is gliding, skiing, or ice skating back to the beginning of the next line: fast yet smooth.

At this point, you are not concerned with comprehension. Your objective is to master the mechanics. For the next few minutes, practice the Quick Start technique in the reading material of your choice until the mechanics begin to feel automatic.

Quick Start: Reading 1

1. Use the same book that you did your initial reading in, but make sure that you read entirely new material. Place a paper clip on the line where you will begin.
2. Read for one minute for as good comprehension as initially, or for even better understanding. The only difference is that this time you will use your index finger to underline as you read. Only go as fast as you can see and understand all the words. Place a second clip on the line where you stop.
3. Estimate your comprehension. Was your comprehension good, fair, or poor? Was it better than, the same as, or worse than in your initial reading?
4. Count the number of lines you read in that one

minute and multiply that number by your average words per line as you determined in Chapter 1. Compare the words per minute of both readings.

Regardless of your results, nothing worth learning is perfect the first time you attempt it. The Quick Start technique will become easier and more comfortable with more practice. During the last reading, you were probably more focused on *what you were doing*, as opposed to the material you were reading. The next time you use the Quick Start you will be a little more relaxed and that in itself will help your concentration and your comprehension.

One other point needs to be reemphasized. You must bring your finger from line to line both quickly and smoothly. The natural tendency of most people is to move their finger from line to line at the same rate as their reading speed. This feels comfortable, but is unnecessary. You can train your finger to respond automatically to the end of a line and zip back to the next line, similar to the way that you've trained your foot to hit the brake when you come to a red light. However, to establish this subconscious reaction requires more practice on your part, starting right now.

Quick Start: Reading 2

1. Either continue reading where you left off or find an entirely new spot. Do not reread any material. Place a paper clip at your beginning spot.
2. Time yourself for one minute using the Quick Start method. Read for as good comprehension as in the last reading, or for even better. Remember to move your finger from line to line as quickly and as smoothly as you can.
3. Place a second clip on the line where you stop. Estimate your comprehension and then determine your words per minute.

Chances are, you felt your comprehension was a little better during the second reading simply because you were a little more comfortable with the mechanics of the Quick Start. Do a few more readings with the Quick Start with the following objectives:

- Comprehension must be as good as or better than in your initial reading.
- The mechanics of the Quick Start method begin to feel more comfortable.
- You move your finger from line to line quickly and smoothly.

How the Quick Start Increases Reading Speed

You may have already doubled your reading speed, or increased it by a third or perhaps by fifty words per minute. But why is there any increase? All you have done differently is used your finger to pace yourself. You're still reading word by word and you're still subvocalizing. Your increase in reading speed is explained by your answer to the following question: When you were counting the lines that you just read, did you let your eyes run down the page all by themselves or did you use your finger, a pencil, or a pen to help you count? There is a high probability that you used one of the pointing devices just mentioned because you wanted to be accurate and didn't want to lose your place. If you think about it, there are really only two ways to be inaccurate: either you can miss a line or you can count the same line twice. Isn't this the same problem as unconscious regression that was discussed earlier? The Quick Start technique reduces regression because your eyes now have a guide, your index finger.

Furthermore, the Quick Start method is just as effective in reducing the problem of slow recovery time. Your eyes return to the beginning of each line faster with a visual guide than by themselves because your eyes are attracted to motion. Next time you're outdoors (or indoors) and out of the corner of your eye you see something move, notice how quickly and instinctively your eyes are drawn to that object. The Quick Start method takes advantage of this natural tendency. As soon as your finger moves to the next line, the motion attracts your eyes' attention. The faster you move your finger, the faster your eyes will move.

Can using the Quick Start really make that much difference in your reading speed? You'd better believe it. Remember that unconscious regression and slow recovery time account for half of the average person's reading time. Consequently, if you eliminate both of these problems, you can easily double your reading speed.

However, it's also important to note that the Quick Start technique has done nothing to help you read groups of words at a time, improve your concentration, or reduce subvocalization significantly. These major reading problems will be addressed next as you're introduced to the true dynamics of speed reading.

Points to Remember

1. Using the hand as a pacer combines the best of the machine and eye movement schools of speed reading without the disadvantages.
2. Using the hand as a visual guide for speed reading
   a. reduces unconscious regression and slow recovery time
   b. allows you to see and read groups of words with each fixation
   c. helps to reduce subvocalization
   d. creates attention on the material
   e. adds rhythm, which activates the right side of your brain
   f. gives you flexibility to adjust reading speed to meet your purpose

3. The Quick Start, which uses the index finger as a pacer, can double your reading speed in an hour by reducing the problems of regression and slow recovery time.

CHAPTER 5 THE KEY TO SPEED READING

Questions to keep in mind: What is the key to speed reading? What is the difference between practicing and reading? What elements are involved in practicing?

To play the game of speed reading, you must start with the basics. In this respect, speed reading is no different than any sport or game. For example, if you were to take your very first tennis lesson you'd be introduced to some of the fundamentals, such as the way to hold the racquet, the differences between a forehand and a backhand swing, and the method of scoring. Only after you have become proficient with the basics of tennis can you focus your attention on learning various game strategies. In speed reading, first you must learn how to break in a book, how to turn pages, and how to use a variety of reading and practice hand motions before you can focus on the mental part of the game, which includes comprehension, concentration, and recall.

LEARNING THE RULES OF THE GAME

1. Breaking in a Book

The first basic of speed reading is learning how to ready a book for high speed drills. This is especially a necessity for paperbacks. Take the front and back covers of the book and run your index fingers as close to the center binding as you can (see Figure 5A). Then, simultaneously separate approximately seven to eight pages from the front and back of the book and again run your index fingers along the center crease. Continue to section off seven to eight pages from front and back as just described until you reach the center of the book. At this point, you'll find it easier to turn pages.

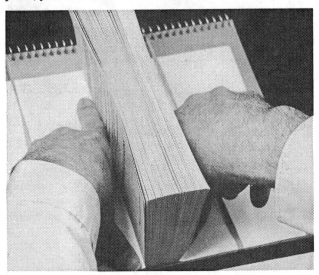

Figure 5A
Breaking in a Book

2. The Thumb and Index Finger Hand Position

The Thumb and Index Finger Hand Position is ultimately more efficient for speed reading than the one-finger Quick Start motion. Your thumb and index finger form an "O" shape, while your other three fingers stay together (see Figure 5B). It looks like an "okay" sign. Your three fingers that are together should be comfortable, not too tight or too loose.

Figure 5B
The Thumb and Index Finger Hand Position

3. The Speed Reading Hand Alternative One

Use the Thumb and Index Finger Hand Position to practice the same underlining technique that you learned in the last chapter (see Figure 5C). To avoid confusion with the Quick Start method, we call this hand motion the Speed Reading Hand Alternative One. Tilt your book slightly on an angle. Focus above your tallest finger or fingers (if two are about the same size). Underline every line from margin to margin. At the end of each line, raise your hand slightly off the page and move it back to the next line as quickly and as smoothly as you can. Make an effort to keep your head stationary and allow your eyes to follow your hand across the line. It is not necessary to move your whole arm back and forth. Simply move your wrist slightly from side to side. If touching the page bothers you, feel free to raise your hand slightly above the page.

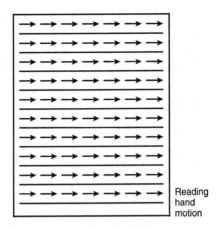

Reading
hand
motion

Figure 5C
The Speed Reading Hand Alternative One

4. The Key to Speed: Practicing

The key to further increasing your reading speed deals with the distinction between the concepts of *reading* and *practicing*. When you are asked to read, you strive for your best comprehension. However, when you practice, you should ignore comprehension and focus on speed.

In speed reading terms, *practicing* means that you are moving at a rate of speed faster than you can possibly comprehend. At any time during a practice exercise, if you start to comprehend, even if it's only 50 percent of the material, you are going too slow.

The main purpose of practicing is to increase your reading speed. The faster you practice, the faster you will ultimately read. However, the basic rule is that you want to practice at a minimum of three times the rate you want to be reading at. If your long-term speed reading objective is to read 1000 w.p.m., your minimum practice rate needs to be 3000 w.p.m. However, that does not mean that you will immediately start practicing at 3000 w.p.m. You will build up to that point gradually, using subgoals and the criteria that will be outlined shortly.

5. Page Turning

In speed reading, each hand has a distinct purpose. The dominant hand becomes the reading or practice hand. The opposite hand is for page-turning. In high-speed practice drills, page turning is often frustrating, but don't allow it to get the best of you. Whenever necessary, use the deep breathing exercise to relax.

Turn pages with your opposite hand, and anticipate the turning of the page. Use your thumb, middle, and index fingers to turn pages from the top right-hand corner. The thumb pushes up on the page on a slight angle to the left. This lifts the page just enough so that you can flip it with your index and middle fingers. If you are left-handed, you can turn pages from either the top or the bottom. Practice page turning for the next few minutes. Make the effort to become more proficient and consistent. Although page turning will never be perfect, it can and will get better.

3-2-1 Practice Drill

Time Frame: 3 minutes

1. Place a paper clip at any beginning spot in your practice book.
2. Use the Thumb and Index Finger Hand Position to pace yourself line by line for three minutes. Underline at a rate of speed faster than you can understand, but be sure that the words are still clear to your vision. If they appear blurred, you are going too fast; if you begin to understand the content of the material, you are going too slow. Focus on the words above your fingertips.

3. Stop and place a clip on the last line completed.

Time Frame: 2 minutes

Every exercise and every reading from this point on will have a very specific goal. Your goal for this next exercise is as follows: you will now cover the same amount of material in only *two minutes*. During this time frame, the words may not be as clear to your vision. At times, you may underline more than one line at a time. None of this is important as long as you get to your ending paper clip in two minutes or less.

1. Return to your first clip where you began the three-minute drill.
2. Cover the same material that you covered in three minutes in only two minutes. Keep your eyes focused above your fingertips and turn pages with the opposite hand. If you reach your second clip early, keep going.

Time Frame: 1 minute

In this one-minute drill, some of the problems described previously may get worse before they get better and here's why. The same material you originally covered in three minutes and then in two, you will now cover in only one minute. In order to get to your ending clip in just sixty seconds, you will have to use a rapid brushing motion. Pretend you are brushing crumbs off the page or quickly painting each page with your fingers. You may underline two or even three lines at a time.

1. Return to your beginning clip.
2. Reach your ending clip in one minute or less.

Common Problems

Here are some of the common problems that people experience when first beginning these practice drills.

1. Eyes and Hand Separate. There will be times when your eyes and your hand separate. Your eyes may stop and stare at a word while your hand keeps moving. The reason for this is that your eyes want to slow down and get more meaning. You're not used to looking at a book where your objective is *not* to comprehend. Eye/hand coordination will continue to improve with more practice.

2. Missing Words. You may feel that you are not seeing every word while doing these high-speed practice exercises. Often you will see more of the words in the center of the page and miss words near the margins. Sometimes the words are blurred or fuzzy.

All of this is quite natural and you should not let it concern you. Remember that you are practicing, not reading, so even if you do miss some of the words it really makes no difference. In any case, you are probably seeing far more of the words than you think. The main reason you feel you're missing so many words is that you are not being given the time to pronounce each word inside your head. You still associate hearing the word with seeing the word. One of the side benefits of these exercises will be to help you reduce the problem of subvocalization by allowing you to get used to seeing words without pronouncing them.

3. Eye and Hand Fatigue. Some people experience eye fatigue initially. If this happens, simply stop and take a break. You may also experience some physical fatigue in your hand or wrist. The speed reading hand methods are a physical approach to reading faster, and some initial fatigue is normal until you adjust.

How Practicing Increases Your Reading Speed

The uncomfortable feeling you experience during high speed practice drills is due to the desire of your eyes and mind to understand the material. They are frantically making their best effort to adjust, but you are constantly pushing them beyond their comfort zone. How does this increase reading speed? Although it may not feel this way, your eyes and mind are doing everything in their power to adjust to the faster rates of speed, but never enough to actually comprehend.

The acclimation of your eyes and mind to the faster rates is similar to what happens to you when you are in your car traveling at a constant rate of speed. Let's assume you are driving on a freeway at a speed of 80 miles per hour. After the first couple of minutes of moving this fast, your body acclimates and the rate of speed doesn't feel too fast or too slow—it just feels normal. Now, if you slow down from 80 miles per hour to 55, what does that feel like? It feels slow, as if you are crawling along, and yet you are still going relatively fast. It only feels slow in comparison to the 80 miles per hour.

This same principle applies to speed reading. By practicing at faster rates, your eyes and mind begin to adjust so that when you slow down to read, your reading rate will be much faster than before. However, your reading rate will not feel fast to you; it will feel comfortable.

The Need for Repetition

Although the primary purpose of practicing is to increase reading speed, a secondary objective is to perfect the mechanics of speed reading. Repetition of practice exercises will allow the basics to become second nature, thus allowing you to place more of your attention on your desired outcome.

Make the effort to have each repetition of a practice exercise be slightly better than the time before. By focusing on small increments of improvement, you will avoid overwhelming frustration and will be much more likely to reach your speed reading goals.

Daily Practice Drills

Repeat the 3-2-1 drill approximately eight to ten times a day for a minimum of a week before you progress to more advanced techniques. After completing each practice session, read for good comprehension for one minute. Determine a reading rate, estimate your comprehension, and record both on your Daily Progress Report Sheet.

Points to Remember

1. Speed reading is similar to a sport in that you have to master certain fundamentals such as breaking in a book, page turning, and hand motions.
2. Practicing is the key to increasing reading speed.
3. You must practice at a minimum of three times the rate you want to be reading at.

CHAPTER 6

PRACTICING: SPEED PLUS RECALL

Questions to keep in mind:
What's a Slash Memory Tree?
What is book control?
How does visualizing help recall?

THE SPEED READING HAND ALTERNATIVE TWO

Once you have mastered Alternative One, you can move to a slightly more advanced hand motion. This second reading hand motion is called the Speed Reading Hand Alternative Two. You still use the Thumb and Index Finger Hand Position and you will still underline every line. However, the difference is that with Alternative One you underlined the entire line from margin to margin whereas with Alternative Two you will underline only the middle third to two-thirds of the line and allow your peripheral vision to see the words at the beginning and ending of each line (see Figure 6A).

Everyone's span of vision is a little bit different and it can even be different from your right eye to your left eye, so here is the way to determine how much of the line you should underline with Alternative Two. Open your practice book to an average page and look at the first word on the first line. Now move on and look at the second word in that line. While looking at the second word can you still see the first word? Chances are that you can; you are using your peripheral vision. Move

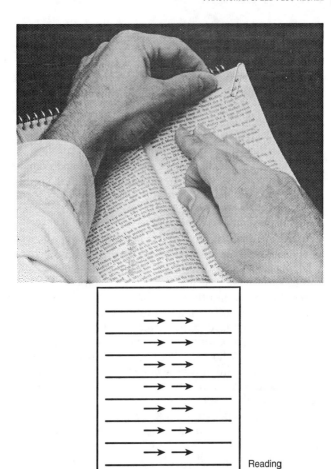

Figure 6A
The Speed Reading Hand Alternative Two

to the third word. Can you still see the first two words? If you can, continue to move to the fourth word and so on.

When you can no longer see all the words clearly, move back to the previous word; that's where you will begin Alternative Two. There's no right or wrong to this: whatever your natural span of vision encompasses will determine how much of the line you underline.

Now that you know your limit on the left margin, you must determine the same for the right. Don't assume that just because you could move in three words on the left it will be the same for the right. It might be more and it might be less. Reverse the process: look at the last word in any average line, and then move to the second word from the end and so on. Remember you must see the words clearly. If they begin to blur, then move back to the previous word.

Why is Alternative Two a faster and more efficient hand motion than Alternative One? Although both hand motions accomplish the purpose of giving your eyes a guide to get them from line to line, Alternative Two gives your eyes a little more freedom to use your natural span of vision to take in more with each fixation. Since you don't have to underline the entire line, it takes less time to get your hand to the next line and since your eyes are following your hand, it also takes them less time. Consequently, you continue to reduce slow recovery time even more with the Speed Reading Hand Alternative Two. Alternative Two is ultimately a few hundred words per minute faster than Alternative One, but does require greater use of your peripheral vision and highly developed eye/hand coordination.

Take a few minutes right now to become familiar with the mechanics of Alternative Two. Determine how much of the line you need to underline in order to see all the words clearly. At this point, you are not to concern yourself with comprehension.

PRACTICE WITH ALTERNATIVE TWO

The 3-2-1 minute speed drill that you used with Alternative One is also used with Alternative Two. However, following are a number of new elements to add to your practice drills.

PRACTICE DRILL ELEMENTS

The Slash Memory Tree

Recall is a skill and like any skill it improves with practice. Starting now, you will add the element of recall to these practice speed drills. However, this does not mean that you are expected to obtain any significant comprehension during these practice sessions. Nonetheless, during this next practice session, you will write down random words and phrases, using a unique note taking tool known as a *Slash Memory Tree* (see Figure 6B).

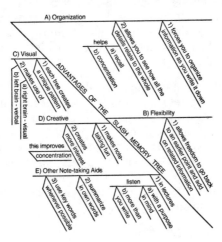

Figure 6B
The Slash Memory Tree

Advantages of the Slash Memory Tree

The Slash Memory Tree is an effective note-taking device for books, meetings, or lectures, which has a number of advantages over the conventional outline form of note taking. A brief summary of some of these advantages follows.

1. Organizes the material. Organization is a key component to a superior memory. The Slash Memory Tree format requires you to categorize information as you write it down. You must decide whether the information is a main idea, a detail, or a supporting idea. The more organized the information is on the way into the mind, the easier it is to recall later.

2. Whole-brain learning. The Slash Memory Tree brings both sides of your brain into the note-taking process. When you write down the information, you activate the left side of your brain. However, the unique pattern of each Slash Memory Tree becomes a visual representation of the material and activates the right side of your brain. The end result is significantly better recall of the information.

3. Flexibility. In outline note taking, you rarely have the flexibility to return to a previous point and add new information. No matter how organized you intend to be, your notes begin to look sloppy as you squeeze information in the margins or draw arrows to connect data.

The Slash Memory Tree gives you the flexibility to build on ideas. The basic design leaves enough space between ideas so that you always have the option to add new information if necessary.

Your Own Memory Tree

On a sheet of paper, draw a long diagonal line dividing the sheet equally into two triangles. This diagonal line is the *trunk* of your Slash Memory Tree. Write the title of your practice book on the trunk.

You're now going to go through a 3-2-1 practice speed drill, but this time you will recall information on your Slash Memory Tree.

3-2-1 Practice Drill

Time Frame: 3 minutes

1. Place a paper clip at your beginning spot.
2. Using Alternative One or Two, practice for three minutes at a rate faster than you can understand, but be sure that the words are clear to your vision. Look for some random words or phrases to add to your Slash Memory Tree.
3. Place a paper clip at your ending spot. Write any information you can recall on your Slash Memory Tree. For example, let's assume you remember two character names and a setting. Each character and the setting are written on separate branches. Always leave room between the branches so that you can add related information later.

Book Control—Becoming an Active Reader

You're now going to add another new element, called *book control*, to the practice speed drills. Book control means that you read the material with specific questions in mind that you want answered. Rather than treat reading as a passive process, you become an active reader. You control the material. You know exactly what you want and you go in to find it.

The concept of book control means that from this point on you will approach all of your reading and practice sessions with a game plan or strategy. Different material will require different strategies. Having a specific purpose helps to improve your concentration, comprehension, and recall for the following reasons:

■ Specific questions create attention on the material.
■ A well-defined purpose makes it easy to find and recall information.

Look at the information you already have written on your Slash Memory Tree and turn that information into specific questions that you want answered. For example, let's assume you wrote *Rick rides horse* on your Slash Memory Tree. What specific questions could you ask? Well, you could ask whether Rick is a cowboy, a farmer, or a circus performer, or whether he rides horses just for recreation. You might want to know the color of his horse. You might ask how old Rick is or how tall he is. There are literally countless questions you could ask, but you need only two or three to establish book control.

Now try the two-minute speed drill.

Time Frame: 2 minutes

1. Return to your beginning paper clip. Review your Slash Memory Tree and have two or three specific questions you want answered.
2. Using Alternative One or Two, reach your ending paper clip in two minutes. You are searching for the answers to your questions, but priority one is still speed.
3. Stop and add any new information to your Slash Memory Tree. Place *new but related* information on *separate but connecting* branches. For example, you determine that Rick is a cowboy, so you write the word *cowboy* on a connecting line underneath *Rick rides horse.* Any new unrelated information gets its own separate branch.

The Difference Between Recognition and Recall

During the two-minute practice exercise, as you went back through the material, you probably noticed many things that you planned to write down last time. However, when you stopped, you still might not have been able to recall the information. See what you can add to the Slash Memory Tree with the one-minute drill.

Time Frame: 1 minute

1. Return to your beginning spot. Look over your Slash Memory Tree and formulate new specific questions you want answered.
2. Using a rapid brushing version of Alternative Two, reach your ending paper clip in one minute. Look for answers to your questions, but most importantly reach your second clip.
3. Stop and add any new information to your Slash Memory Tree, even if it's only a word or two. The key is to make the effort. Recall will continue to improve with repetition.

Visualization

There's one last element to add to these practice drills and then you'll have all the basics in place. The final element is visualization. From this point on, whether practicing or reading, try to make a mental picture of whatever you are seeing on the page. By visualizing, you will improve your ability to concentrate and recall information, for the following reasons:

1. Picture Better Concentration. Visualizing creates attention on the material, which is an essential element of good concentration. Even if you are reading abstract material that is difficult to picture, just making the effort to visualize will improve concentration. Why? In order to come to the conclusion that something is too abstract to visualize, your mind has to focus on the material to begin with.

2. Bye-Bye Daydreams. Visualize as you read and you bring the right part of your brain into the reading process. Reading is predominantly a left brain activity because it deals with language. That doesn't mean the right hemisphere can't participate. The right hemisphere of your brain has a biological need to make pictures. This is why you often daydream while you read. Your right brain is essentially telling you, "Okay, if you're not going to allow me to play, I'll think about what I did yesterday, or I'll think about what I'll do tomorrow or that movie I saw last night." Conversely, by making the effort to visualize while you read, you transform the right side of your brain into a positive and potent ally that will enhance both your recall and your concentration.

3. A Picture Is Worth a Thousand Words. Visualizing improves memory. Studies in psychology have proven that we remember pictures better than we do words and that visual memory is longer lasting than verbal memory. In one study, subjects were shown more than ten thousand photographs and there was a recognition factor of over 99 percent.

Points to Remember

1. Recall is a skill that can be developed with practice.
2. The Slash Memory Tree is a unique method of note taking that
   a. organizes information
   b. uses both sides of your brain
   c. improves memory
3. Book Control
   a. creates attention on the material
   b. makes you active in the reading process
   c. trains you to read with a purpose in mind
4. Visualization
   a. creates attention on the material
   b. brings the right side of your brain into the reading process
   c. improves memory

CHAPTER 7

OPENING YOUR FOCUS

Questions to keep in mind: How does an open focus increase reading speed? What are the purposes of the Question Mark, the Horseshoe, and the Tracer hand motions and how do they differ?

Reading groups of words with each fixation of your eyes is one of the essential skills of an advanced speed reader. Not only will reading groups of words increase your reading speed, but it will improve your concentration and comprehension. However, you cannot read groups of words until you can see groups of words. That is why retraining your eyes to see the page in a new way is the first step. There are a number of hand motions and practice exercises to help you utilize more of your natural vision when you read or practice.

THE QUESTION MARK HAND MOTION

The Question Mark is a practice hand motion and will never be used to read with. It's called the Question Mark because that's exactly what it looks like (see Figure 7A). Using the Thumb and Index Finger Hand Position, trace a large question mark down each page in your practice book. Turn pages with the opposite hand. The Question Mark Hand Motion is done quickly, approximately one second per page.

The main objectives of the Question Mark are to start to relax your focus and to develop better eye/hand

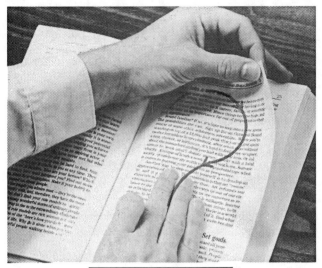

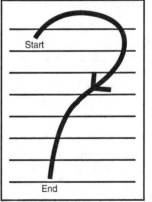

Figure 7A
The Question Mark Practice Hand Motion

coordination. Take a few minutes to practice and become comfortable with the mechanics of the Question Mark.

Question Mark Exercise

1. Place a paper clip on page 60 of your practice book and then return to the first page.
2. You have one minute to cover 60 pages using the Question Mark Hand Motion. It's a very fast motion, approximately one second per page.
3. Pretend your hand is covered in wet black ink or paint and you're tracing a question mark down each page. Turn pages with your opposite hand.
4. Repeat five more times. Each time try to make your effort just a little bit better: better eye/hand coordination, better page turning, and a smoother hand motion.

Your main objective is eye/hand coordination, so watch that trail you're leaving behind with each Question Mark.

Two Common Questions

1. What are my eyes supposed to be doing?
Your eyes are following your hand. Pretend your hand is covered in wet black paint or ink, and you're watching the trail that you'd leave if you traced a large question mark on each and every page. Allow your eyes to relax. Forget about individual words. See whole areas of the page.

2. Page turning is difficult. What can I do?
Anticipate the turning of the page. If you turn more than one page at a time, don't concern yourself with separating pages, just keep on going. Page turning will improve with repetition, but it will never be perfect. Don't allow it to frustrate you.

THE HORSESHOE OR "U" HAND MOTION

The objective of the Horseshoe or "U" practice hand motion is to see the entire page as if it were nothing more than an abstract painting, a picture, or a design. In other words, you want to see the entire page as a whole. The hand motion is called the Horseshoe or "U" because that's exactly what it looks like, and it is one of the most unusual of all the hand motions you will learn. First of all, whether you are right-handed or left-handed, for this particular hand motion you will use your left hand to form the Horseshoe and you will turn pages with your right hand. The second unusual thing about the Horseshoe is that you do not start on the left page but on the right, and you will finish on the left (see Figure 7B). Using the Thumb and Index Finger position with your left hand, bring your hand quickly down the right hand page, tracing half of a large capital "U". When you get to the bottom of the page, flip your wrist, and complete the rest of the "U" up the left page. You move down the right page and up the left in a fast fluid motion and, as with the Question Mark, you must anticipate page turning.

At this point, don't concern yourself with the purpose of the Horseshoe technique. Instead concentrate on mastering the mechanics until they begin to feel comfortable or automatic. Only at that point should you concern yourself with the hand motion's real objective. Also, the Horseshoe will be a little easier if you practice in a hardcover book as opposed to a paperback. Page turning can often become frustrating and this is especially true when you practice with a paperback. In any case, do not concern yourself if you occasionally turn more than one page at a time. Take a few minutes and practice the mechanics of the Horseshoe Hand Motion.

You may still be concerned about what your eyes are supposed to focus on. Unlike the Question Mark, where your objective was to methodically follow the invisible trail of ink that your hand was tracing out, the Horseshoe motion is twice as fast and your hand should move almost like a flash from a camera, click down the one side, click up the other. Your eyes are the camera.

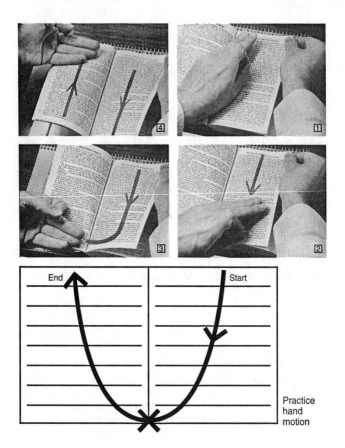

Figure 7B
The Horseshoe or "U" Practice Hand Motion

You want to see the whole page in a single glance. This doesn't mean you will understand what is on the page. You simply want to see the whole as a shape or design.

The Horseshoe is an excellent warm-up exercise. In the same way that a runner stretches before jogging, you should use the Horseshoe for a few minutes anytime before you begin to read or practice. Not only will the Horseshoe help to open up your focus, but it's the fastest of all the hand motions. Any drill or reading that you do after the Horseshoe will seem slower.

Horseshoe Practice Exercise

Time Frame: 2 minutes
Practice the Horseshoe Hand Motion in a book of your choice. See the entire page as a picture or a design. Repeat five times, making each time a little bit better than the last.

THE TRACER HAND MOTION

The Tracer Hand Motion is also designed to increase your span of vision, but in a different way than the Horseshoe or Question Mark. The Tracer's purpose is for you to see three to five lines as a solid block or a small picture or design. Comprehension is a non-issue with the Tracer. It is a practice hand motion to help retrain your eyes to see areas of print. The mechanics of the Tracer allow you the option of using either the Thumb and Index Finger Hand Position or just your index finger. Either way you will trace out three- to five-line sections of the page (see Figure 7C). Pretend your fingers are a pencil or marker blocking off small sections all the way down the page. Trace out three- to five-line sections in a smooth, continuous motion all the way down each page without skipping any lines. Practice the Tracer until the mechanics feel comfortable.

To clarify what you want to see with the Tracer, find a page in your practice book that has quite a few smaller paragraphs and then turn the page upside down. At this point, you can see each of the smaller paragraphs as if they were solid blocks or wholes. Now, use the Tracer down the page and continue to see each small paragraph as a whole. That's what you want to see when you flip the book right side up.

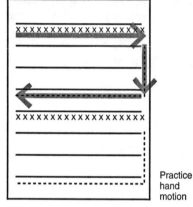

Practice
hand
motion

Figure 7C
The Tracer Practice Hand Motion

The main problem you will most likely encounter with the Tracer is that most paragraphs are not uniform in size and often encompass more than three to five lines. In larger paragraphs you have to create your own three- to five-line boundaries by using the Tracer motion.

Keep the hand motion smooth and consistent. In fact, think in terms of sectioning out the same amount of space each time. As you trace out each three- to five-line section, make the effort to see those lines as a solid block or a whole. Let your eyes relax. It's not important that you feel as if you are seeing each and every word.

Often the areas of print seem blurred. At times you may see more than three to five lines. That's fine. It doesn't have to be that precise. The key is to make the effort to see small blocks of print each time.

Tracer Practice Exercise/5-3-2 Drill

Time Frame: 5 minutes

1. Place a paper clip at a beginning spot in your practice book.
2. Practice for five minutes using the Tracer to section out three to five lines each time. Make the effort to see each section as a whole.
3. Stop and place an ending paper clip in the book.

Time Frame: 3 minutes

1. Go back to your beginning clip.
2. You have three minutes to cover the same material. It will be necessary for you to take in more lines with each Tracer motion. For example, you might section out seven to eight lines rather than three to five.
3. Your primary objective is to allow your eyes to relax to see the larger areas of print with each Tracer motion.

Time Frame: 2 Minutes

1. Return to your beginning clip.
2. Because you now have only two minutes, you will need to take in even larger sections of print, perhaps dividing the page into thirds or in half.
3. Remember that comprehension is not your objective. This is strictly a visual exercise.

SEEING AND READING GROUPS OF WORDS

You are now going to go back and use either Alternative One or Alternative Two to divide each line into thirds and possibly halves, depending upon your peripheral vision. With the Horseshoe hand motion, your objective is to see the entire *page* as a whole; with the Tracer, your objective is to see three to five *lines* as a small block of print. Now, your new objective is to see only three to five *words* with each fixation of your eyes.

In this section, you will practice dividing each line into thirds. Using the Speed Reading Hand Alternative One or Two, let your eyes relax to see a third of each line with each fixation of your eyes. It's not important that you comprehend the words you are seeing. The point of this exercise is to retrain your eyes to see groups of words with each fixation of your eyes. Once this begins to feel comfortable, you will automatically begin to group words together in complete units or ideas. It's the way your mind naturally works. When you look at a clock, you don't think *numbers; big hand; little hand; oh, that must be a clock*. You see it as a whole, right from the start. In truth, you already use this concept when you read individual words. When you first learned to read, you began with the alphabet. You took individual letters and put them together to form words: c, a, t, cat, d, o, g, dog. Do you still have to break these words into letters, or do you see *cat* and *dog* as complete words? Of course you do, but that's where your training stopped long ago. Your next step now is to first see and then read three, four, or five words at a time as a complete unit of thought.

Visual Exercise

Make the effort to see and read these phrases in one fixation of your eyes:

a red apple   a little old man   a ringing telephone
a bright blue sweater   a noisy alarm clock
a color computer monitor   a twelve-month desk calendar
a digital microwave oven   a professional baseball player
a ten-story office building   a tall, shady elm tree
an electric pencil sharpener

CHAPTER 8

ADVANCED SPEED READING DRILLS

Questions to keep in mind: What elements should be included in all speed reading drills? What is the purpose of warm-up exercises? What are add-a-page speed drills and how do they increase reading speed?

The exercises and drills in this chapter have been designed to help you continue to build reading speed and comprehension while allowing the mechanics of speed reading to become automatic or subconscious. There are three separate drill sessions that should be alternated daily. Practice a minimum of 45 minutes to an hour a day for the next six weeks. Your one overall goal is that each time you repeat an exercise it will be a little bit better than the time before.

Time Yourself with a Cassette Player

Although you can use a watch with a secondhand or even a stopwatch, the best way to time yourself for longer practice sessions is to use an audiocassette recorder/player. Place a blank cassette in your recorder. Start to record while keeping track of the time. When a minute is up, speak into the recorder and say, "one minute," and continue to do this every minute until you have a ten-minute drill tape or longer (you can always rewind). Now play the tape whenever you practice and you will be able to place more of your attention on the drills.

PRACTICE SESSION ONE

Warm-up Drill/Question Mark Hand Motion

Purpose: To develop eye/hand coordination and to open focus

Time Frame: 2 Minutes

1. Place a paper clip on page 120 of your practice book and then turn back to page 1.
2. Using the Question Mark Hand Motion, attempt to cover a page a second for two minutes. Pretend your hand is covered in wet ink or paint. Watch the invisible trail you're leaving behind.

Repeat three times.

Speed Drills

All speed drills include the following procedures:

1. On a sheet of paper set up a Slash Memory Tree with the title of the book on the trunk of the tree.
2. Practice at a minimum of three times the rate of your short-term reading goal.
3. Visualize as you practice to activate your right brain.
4. At the end of each practice session write information you recall on your Slash Memory Tree.
5. Turn what you write into mental questions, so you can actively search for the information in the next practice session.

Objectives:

- Priority One is speed. Get to your paper clip at the end of the designated time frame.
- The secondary purpose is to sharpen your skills of visualization and book control.
- The third objective is to continue to perfect the mechanics of speed reading.

3-2-1 Drill

Time Frame: 3 minutes

1. Place a paper clip at your beginning point. Practice for three minutes using the Speed Reading Hand Alternative One or Alternative Two. Focus above your fingertips. Move your hand and eyes faster than you can understand, but be sure the words are clear to your vision. Visualize and look for some main ideas to write on your Slash Memory Tree.

2. Stop and place a second paper clip at your ending spot. Recall on your Slash Memory Tree, leaving room so you can add new information later. Begin to formulate specific questions to answer during the next time frame.

Time Frame: 2 minutes

1. Cover the same material in two minutes. Visualize and look for answers to questions.

2. Stop and add to your Slash Memory Tree. Formulate new questions.

Time Frame: 1 minute

1. Using a rapid brushing version of Alternative One or Two, cover the same material in only one minute. Words may sometimes blur and you may feel that you're seeing more words in the center of the page. Visualize and look for answers to your questions.

2. Stop and add to your Slash Memory Tree.

Repeat the 3-2-1 Drill five times.

How to Determine Your Practice Rate

After the three-minute time frame of the fifth repetition, calculate a practice rate and record it on your Daily Progress Report Sheet. Remember you should practice at a minimum of three times the rate you want to be reading at. Use the procedure described in Chapter 1 to determine your daily practice rate.

Reading Drills

Prepare to Speed Read. Anytime you sit down to read for good comprehension follow this procedure:

- Relax: use the deep-breathing exercise.
- Tell yourself specifically what you want out of the material (left brain).
- Visualize the desired result (right brain).

Push Reading Drill

Time Frame: 1 minute

1. Place a paper clip at your beginning spot. Using either Speed Reading Hand Alternative One or Alternative Two, read one minute for good comprehension.
2. Stop and place an ending paper clip. Estimate a percentage of comprehension, summarize information on your Slash Memory Tree, and then calculate an approximate w.p.m. (see Chapter 1).
3. Using paper clips, mark off a section in new material that is twice the w.p.m you calculated in Step 2. Again, read for one minute. Keep your comprehension as high as you can while at the same time finishing the section. Add to your Slash Memory Tree. Repeat this procedure two more times, each time doubling the previous w.p.m.
4. In new material, without any set number of pages, read again for one minute for your best comprehension. Estimate your comprehension and calculate your w.p.m. Record on your Daily Progress Report Sheet.

PRACTICE SESSION TWO

Warm-up Exercise/Horseshoe Hand Motion

Purpose: To see each page as if it were an abstract picture; to note the structure of the book (i.e., subtitles, summaries, index, glossary)

Time Frame: 2 minutes

1. Place a clip on page 240 of your book, then turn back to page 1.
2. Moving at a half second per page and using the Horseshoe Hand Motion, cover 240 pages in two minutes. Relax your vision. See each page as a whole.

Repeat three times.

5-3-2 Drill/Tracer Hand Motion

Purpose: To train your eyes to see larger areas of print with each fixation

Time Frame: 5 minutes

1. Place a clip at the beginning of any chapter.
2. Practice for five minutes using the Tracer Hand Motion. Use your fingers to section off three to five lines with each motion. Make the effort to see each section as a solid block or a small picture. Place a paper clip on the line where you stop.
3. Return to your first paper clip. The same material you covered in five minutes, you will now cover in three minutes. You must increase the number of lines you trace around with each hand motion. If it was three to four lines last time, this time you'll section off six or seven lines.
4. Return to your beginning clip. The same material you covered last time in three minutes, you will now cover in two minutes. You'll need to trace out even larger sections this time, perhaps a third to a half of the page

at a time. Allow your vision to relax. See each section as a solid block or a picture.

Repeat the 5-3-2 Drill three times.

PRACTICING FOR SPEED

Add-a-Page Speed Drill

Time Frame: 1 minute

1. Place a paper clip at your beginning spot.
2. Practice with Speed Reading Hand Alternative Two for one minute, at a rate of speed faster than you can understand with the words still clear to your vision. Visualize. Look for main ideas to write on your Slash Memory Tree.
3. At the end of the minute, place a paper clip on the line where you stopped. Recall information on your Slash Memory Tree. Formulate mental questions.
4. Move your ending paper clip forward by two numbered pages (i.e., if you ended on page 50, move your clip to page 52).
5. Return to your beginning clip. Cover the same material, plus the two added pages, in one minute. Use a brushing motion, if necessary, to get there.
6. Stop and add to your Slash Memory Tree.

Repeat this drill twice more, each time adding two pages.

Push Reading Drill

Time Frame: 1 minute

1. Place a paper clip at your beginning spot. Using either the Speed Reading Hand Alternative One or Alternative Two, read one minute for good comprehension.
2. Stop and place an ending paper clip. Estimate a percentage of comprehension, summarize information on your Slash Memory Tree, and then calculate an approximate w.p.m. (see Chapter 1).

3. Using paper clips, mark off a section in new material that is twice the w.p.m you calculated in Step 2. Again, read for one minute. Keep your comprehension as high as you can while at the same time finishing the section. Add to your Slash Memory Tree. Repeat this procedure two more times, each time doubling the previous w.p.m.

4. In new material, without any set number of pages, read again for one minute for your best comprehension. Estimate your comprehension and calculate your w.p.m. Record on your Daily Progress Report Sheet.

PRACTICE SESSION THREE

Warm-up Exercises

1. Question Mark Hand Motion

Time Frame: 2 minutes
Cover a minimum of 120 pages. (For more detailed directions, see p. 69.)

2. Horseshoe Hand Motion

Time Frame: 2 minutes
Cover a minimum of 240 pages. (For more detailed directions, see p. 72.)

Visual Exercise

Tracer Hand Motion/5-3-2 Drill

Time Frame: 5 minutes

1. Place a paper clip at the beginning of any chapter.
2. Practice for five minutes using the Tracer Hand Motion. Place a paper clip on the line where you stop.

Time Frame: 3 minutes

1. Return to your first paper clip.
2. The same material you covered in five minutes, you will now cover in three minutes.

Time Frame: 2 minutes

1. Return to your beginning paper clip.
2. The same material you covered last time in three minutes, you will now cover in two minutes.

Repeat this drill only once.

Advanced Add-a-Page Speed Drill

Time Frame: 1 minute

1. Place a paper clip at your beginning spot.
2. Practice with Speed Reading Hand Alternative Two for one minute, at a rate of speed faster than you can understand with the words still clear to your vision. Visualize. Look for main ideas to write on your Slash Memory Tree. Compute a practice rate.
3. At the end of the minute, place a paper clip on the line where you stopped. Recall information on your Slash Memory Tree. Formulate mental questions.
4. Move your ending paper clip forward by five numbered pages (i.e., if you ended on page 50, move your clip to page 55).
5. Return to your beginning clip. Cover the same material, plus the five added pages, in one minute. Use a brushing motion, if necessary, to get there.

Repeat this drill twice more, each time adding five pages. Each week of practice add an additional page to this exercise. For example, in week two add six pages and in week three add seven pages, until you reach a maximum of ten pages.

Push Reading Drill

Time Frame: 1 minute

1. Place a paper clip at your beginning spot. Using either the Speed Reading Hand Alternative One or Alternative Two, read one minute for good comprehension.

2. Stop and place an ending paper clip. Estimate a percentage of comprehension, summarize information on your Slash Memory Tree, and then calculate an approximate w.p.m.

3. Using paper clips, mark off a section in new material that is twice the w.p.m you calculated in Step 2. Again, read for one minute. Keep your comprehension as high as you can while at the same time finishing the section. Add to your Slash Memory Tree. Repeat this procedure two more times, each time doubling the previous w.p.m.

4. In new material, without any set number of pages, read again for one minute for your best comprehension. Estimate your comprehension and calculate your w.p.m. Record on your Daily Progress Report Sheet.

CHAPTER 9

CONCENTRATION: THE AAIRR FORMULA

Questions to keep in mind: Is concentration innate? What does AAIRR stand for?

In most sports, there is a point where the mental part of the game becomes more important than the physical. This is also true of speed reading. The key to understanding and recalling information at faster rates of speed depends on your ability to concentrate. As was discussed in Chapter 3, lack of concentration is one of the six major reading problems. You cannot have comprehension without concentration because how can you understand what you never had your mind on to begin with?

Concentration involves only one-pointed thought. It's one thing and one thing only on your mind. Good concentration is not something you are necessarily born with or without. Concentration is a skill and like any skill it improves with the proper instruction and practice. To improve your ability to concentrate, you must first understand what positive and negative factors presently determine your ability to focus your mind. All of this information is in the AAIRR (pronounced "air") concentration formula. AAIRR is an acronym that stands for *attitude, attention, interest, relaxation,* and *repetition.* All of these elements must be present simultaneously for you to experience your best concentration.

ATTITUDE

The first element of good concentration is having the proper attitude or mind-set. Many times we sabotage our ability to concentrate by unconsciously telling ourselves what we don't want. For example, you may sit down with some long, difficult technical material and think, "I hate this material; it's so boring. I'm going to sit here all day and I'm still not going to understand it." How can you possibly have your best concentration with this type of negative narrative running through your head?

You must be aware of what you say to yourself before you read or study, because you are a suggestible being. All human beings are suggestible to some degree. Being suggestible simply means that you allow ideas to change your beliefs or behavior. If you were not suggestible, then you would be incapable of learning. Therefore, you want to consciously decide what you say to yourself. In essence, before reading, you need to psyche yourself just as an athlete does when getting ready to play in a big game. You must tell yourself such things as: "My brain is powerful and I control it; I have good concentration and recall; I am a super speed reader with excellent concentration and comprehension."

However, verbal affirmations only activate the left hemisphere of your brain. To involve the right hemisphere, you must simultaneously visualize the benefits of your affirmations. Tell yourself that you are a super speed reader with excellent concentration, but also picture yourself moving through the material totally absorbed, with a look of confidence on your face. Visualize yourself writing all the main points on a sheet of paper and then using that information, whether it be for a presentation, an exam, or simply making interesting conversation at a business luncheon. See the end result clearly and vividly and add as many details as you can to your mental pictures.

Here are some other factors that will make your suggestions and mental pictures more effective:

1. Positive Direct Wording

To make your suggestions more effective, word them in a direct, positive way such as *I am, I can, I shall,* and *I will.* Do not use words that suggest doubt such as *should, maybe,* or *try,* or negatives such as *can't,* or *won't.* For example, if you were giving affirmations to improve your self-confidence, you might say, "I am a confident person. Every day my self-confidence grows stronger and stronger." A negative affirmation would be: "Every day I won't be afraid and I won't listen to other people's doubts about myself." In the latter, the focus is on the problem and only the problem is being reinforced. The key is to keep your mind *on* what you want and *off* what you don't want.

2. Desire and Emotions

Strong desire along with positive emotions will generate the necessary fuel to make your affirmations come alive. Along with your verbal affirmations and visualization, think about how you will feel when you reach your goal. Feel the elation, the confidence, and the pride that come with self-direction. An excellent way to help generate these feelings is to draw upon emotional memories associated with a past success. The past success does not have to be large in scope. It can be something as simple as winning a tennis match or answering a question correctly. The feelings are what are important. If you felt successful at the time, bring back those same emotions.

3. Relaxed Doing

Avoid constant testing of whether or not you are getting the desired results after each time you give yourself affirmations. You have to relax and accept as fact that your results are guaranteed as long as you continue to focus your mind on what you want. If you check constantly for progress, you are in essence telling yourself that you have doubts that this positive attitude approach is working. Emil Coué, the famous French advocate of autosuggestion, called this the Law of Reversed Effect. It simply means that when you are in doubt about something, the harder you try, the harder it becomes. We often use terms to describe this state such as "He's pressing" or "She's trying too hard." You should use the attitude affirmations, knowing they will work, without constantly testing them.

4. Repetition and Relaxation

Repetition and relaxation are two components of the AAIRR concentration formula, and they will be covered in more detail shortly. However, at this juncture, it is important to discuss briefly the importance of these elements in relation to attitude.

The more relaxed you are when you give yourself verbal or visual suggestions, the more likely they will take effect. As the body relaxes, less of the mind's energy is diverted toward it, thus freeing more energy to focus on your affirmations. Make it a habit to use either the diaphragm deep-breathing exercise, or another relaxation exercise that you'll be learning later in this chapter, before giving yourself any positive affirmations.

Repetition is the single most important element that determines whether an affirmation or mental picture is accepted as true by the mind. In fact, repetitions of verbal and visual affirmations shape the mind, just as repetitions of physical exercises shape the body. However, you can't expect to see results the very first time you give yourself positive affirmations, just as you would not expect your biceps to bulge after one barbell curl. It may take hundreds or even thousands of repetitions over a period of time before you see any significant results. Repetitions of mental affirmations work exactly the same way. Over time, you will see a cumulative effect as you shape your mind to become the person you want to be.

ATTENTION

The next element of our AAIRR concentration formula is attention. Attention is simply the placement or direction of your mental focus. For example, you can't possibly have your attention on reading a book if you're watching television. Anything that takes your attention away from the activity you attempt to concentrate on is a distraction. These distractions can be either internal or external. By learning how to eliminate or reduce these distractions, you can significantly improve your concentration.

Eliminate External Distractions

To eliminate external distractions, you need to create an environment that is conducive to good concentration. For example, when reading or studying, you need good lighting that doesn't distract with shadows or glare that can cause eyestrain. You also need a comfortable chair and a desk or table that is the right height for you. Avoid sitting near potential distractions such as the telephone, television, radio, or friends or coworkers who are socializing when you need to focus. You also want to eliminate as much external noise as possible. Sometimes this is not within your control. Obviously you can't always control the noise factor from family members or coworkers, but it is possible to create your own background sounds that potentially help concentration. Studies in neuropsychology have proven that the largo movements of baroque music played at one beat per second correspond to the natural rhythm of the human body and stimulate learning and improve concentration. If silence is not possible, either play this music in the background or listen with headphones. This is discussed in more detail under *relaxation* in the AAIRR formula.

Another common external distraction to concentration is lack of organization. Before you begin to read or work, make sure you have all the proper tools within reach. Clutter or a disorganized work space is a distraction to the mind. For example, let's assume you have four separate reading assignments to finish in a given day. You do not want to have all the books and various materials scattered about your desk at the same time. The only thing that should be in front of you is the assignment that you are presently working on. When you finish, move it off your desk, and bring up the next assignment. Otherwise, if you keep all of your books and materials in front of you, you are constantly distracted by the amount of material you still have to do. Organization helps you to focus your attention on the one thing you are presently doing.

Eliminate Internal Distractions

Internal distractions to concentration, such as worry and fear, are far more difficult to control than the external factors. Worry and fear take your mind off your objective and focus your thoughts on the opposite result. For instance, if you are a baseball player and you think, "Gee, I hope I don't strike out," more often than not, that's when you strike out. If you're reading a business journal article and think, "I hope I understand this information," you are taking your mind off the material and therefore you cannot possibly get the result you desire. When people first learn speed reading, their greatest fear is that they may miss something by going too fast. Consequently, by focusing on that fear they create a self-fulfilling prophecy by taking their mind off the material and placing it on the opposite result. To overcome worry and fear, you must apply the AAIRR formula that you are presently learning. Start by establishing the proper attitude. Then set a specific goal, relax, and let go. Letting go means that you stay in the present moment and do not analyze your performance while you are still performing. For example, the best stage actors become the characters they are playing while performing. If they are worrying about whether they will forget their lines or will get bad reviews while they are on stage, chances are that both of these fears will become reality. How can they possibly give their best performance if they are focusing on their fears and not on being the characters they are playing?

So how then do you eliminate worry and fear when you are speed reading or performing any other task? First, you must learn to relax, using either the deep breathing exercise or any other relaxation technique. Second, you must give your mind a specific, realistic goal using positive pictures, words, and emotions. Third, you should do enough repetition, both physical and mental, that the basics of a skill such as speed reading become automatic or second nature. This frees the mind to focus all of its energy on the completion of your goal.

Although concentration is certainly a mental process, your physical state has a lot to do with whether you keep your mind on what you are doing. Concentration should be thought of in holistic terms, where your mind and body work together in harmony. Often the opposite occurs. For example, if you really need to concentrate and you've only had three hours of sleep, yet you require eight hours to be at your best, then your mind and body are in conflict. Similarly, if you eat junk food all day long and expect to have your best concentration, you are only fooling yourself. Concentration requires energy and much of that energy is supplied by your physical body. Abuse your body and it will affect your ability to concentrate.

Briefly, here are some of the essential nutrients needed for good concentration. Choline is one of the most important nutrients for good concentration and memory. It is found in lecithin, which is sold in health food stores, as well as soybeans, in which it occurs naturally. Another essential nutrient for proper brain functioning is folic acid. A deficit of folic acid results in difficulty in both concentration and retention. Folic acid is found in green leafy vegetables such as spinach, parsley, and broccoli. Vitamin C is necessary to reduce stress and remove toxins from the body such as lead and mercury that can affect your ability to concentrate. Vitamin B_3, also known as niacin, is important in helping to maintain the brain's metabolism. Also, vitamins B_6 and B_{12} as well as iron, copper, and zinc are necessary for good concentration, memory, and emotional stability. For more information regarding what foods contain these essential vitamins and nutrients, refer to the chart in Chapter 11.

Another important physiological component to good concentration is your internal body clock. All people have certain times of the day where they are more alert and have more mental and physical energy. Some are morning people while others do their best internal work late at night. Unfortunately, many people ignore their internal body clocks. For example, there are people who concentrate better in the early morning, but instead of using this time for their most strenuous mental work, they read the morning newspaper, socialize with fellow employees, or open their mail. Don't let this happen to you. Discover your best internal times and then religiously schedule activities that require your best concentration.

INTEREST

The third element in our concentration AAIRR formula is interest. Interest is the fuel for good concentration. You probably already realize that it is easier to concentrate on an activity or a subject you are interested in as opposed to something you are not. For example, you will no doubt find it easier to read an entertaining spy novel than a research report. However, often at work you are faced with an assignment that you have little natural interest in. What do you do then? The answer is to replace the word interest with motivation. Ask yourself, "What else about this subject would motivate me to complete the project?" For example, let's assume you have to make a presentation at work and you have little interest in the subject. You have to find something else about the subject or the situation to motivate you. Perhaps a good presentation might mean a promotion, and if that motivates you, then that's what you focus your mind on. Only you can determine what will motivate you when interest isn't present, and then use that motivation to generate the energy necessary for good concentration.

RELAXATION

The fourth element in our AAIRR concentration is relaxation. There are a number of reasons why relaxation is a necessary component of good concentration. First, when the body relaxes, more of your mental energy can be directed to the task at hand. Why? Because whether or not you realize it, your body is the biggest distraction that your mind has to deal with. For example, have you ever tried to concentrate when you have a headache? It's difficult, isn't it? The reason for this goes back to our AAIRR formula. Your attention and interest, two essential elements of good concentration, focus on the pain and not on your objective. Similarly, when your body is tense, it draws energy from your mind and places it on itself. Conversely, the more relaxed your body is, the more energy you have to place on the real focus of your attention.

Relaxation is essential in controlling the internal distractions of stress and worry. An anxious body produces an anxious mind and a relaxed body produces a relaxed mind. A good example of this process is a phenomenon often termed *exam panic*. You study for an exam and arrive at the test site confident that you know the material. You read the first question and you don't know the answer. Suddenly, you start to panic. Now, even information you knew perfectly the night before you can't recall. Time is running out; beads of perspiration begin to form on your forehead. The harder you try to recall the information, the further it slips away. Time is up and you know that you've blown the exam. After the test, you walk into the hallway and suddenly, like a dam bursting, all of the information you forgot just a short time ago comes flooding back. Why? Simply because you have relaxed.

Furthermore, excessive stress can affect your normal breathing pattern and reduce the amount of oxygen that reaches your brain. Getting enough oxygen to the brain is essential for good concentration. Even though the brain makes up only 2 to 3 percent of the body's weight, it requires 25 percent of the body's oxygen supply. One of the best ways both to reduce stress and to increase the brain's oxygen supply is to do some form of physical exercise on a daily basis. Not only will you be healthier, but you'll be able to concentrate better. Another way to reduce stress and increase the oxygen supply to the brain is to use the diaphragm deep-breathing exercise discussed earlier. Below you will find a new relaxation exercise to reduce stress and improve your ability to concentrate.

Melting Snowman Exercise

The Melting Snowman Exercise combines rhythmic deep breathing with visualization to improve your ability to concentrate. With your eyes closed, visualize a snowman. To make your snowman as vivid as possible, exaggerate the image: it can be as large as a mountain, it can be composed of multicolored snow, it can have the face of a good friend of yours, and it can be dressed in the wildest outfit you can imagine. The clearer and more vivid the image, the better. While you visualize your snowman, count backward from fifty to zero. With each count, see your snowman gradually melting, until by the time you reach zero your snowman is nothing more than a puddle of water with all of its clothes lying on the ground. Do the exercise now.

There are numerous things you may have noticed at the conclusion of the Melting Snowman Exercise. See if you can relate to the following. Chances are, you could only keep the image of the snowman clear and vivid for a short period of time—maybe five or ten counts before it faded out. Also, you probably noticed that the exercise filled your mind and you really couldn't think of too much else while you were doing it. Finally, at the end of the exercise you may have noticed that you were physically relaxed. If you didn't experience this, do the exercise a few more times and almost certainly you will find yourself relaxed.

So what does the Melting Snowman Exercise have to do with improving concentration? First, the exercise fills up the mind, thus also clearing the mind. In any given day, you need to concentrate on many different, unrelated activities or projects. Unfortunately, you can't always click off the project you were just working on when starting something new, and, therefore, this prior activity becomes a distraction to what you are presently working on. By using the Melting Snowman Exercise between projects and activities, you start fresh. You clear the mind and minimize the interference of unrelated thoughts.

A second benefit of the Melting Snowman Exercise is that it helps you to relax naturally. The exercise can be used any time you need to relax to give your best performance. But why does it help you to relax? The reason is that it utilizes both sides of your brain. When you visualize, you use the right hemisphere, and when you count, you use the left. In fact, if you think about it, the Melting Snowman Exercise is very similar to the old remedy of people counting sheep to help themselves fall asleep. The fact is that counting sheep actually worked for many people, even though at the time they did not know the reason why. By visualizing the sheep, the right brain was activated, and by counting, the left brain became involved. The combination filled the mind and cleared it from the day's activities and anxieties that kept people from being able to relax and, therefore, sleep. The Melting Snowman Exercise is an improvement because it requires greater involvement of the mind. Counting backward is more difficult than counting forward, and visualizing a constantly changing image of a melting snowman is more involving than a consistent one of jumping sheep.

One way you can use the Melting Snowman Exercise to strengthen your ability to concentrate is to practice keeping the image clear and gradually melting for progressively longer periods of time by using realistic subgoals. For example, let's assume the first time you did the exercise you could only keep the snowman clear and gradually melting for a count of five and then it faded out. Your first subgoal will then be to keep the image clear and melting for a count of ten. When you reach ten, reset it to a count of fifteen, then twenty and so on until you can keep the image of the snowman gradually melting for the entire fifty counts. This one simple exercise can discipline your mind, sharpen your visualization skills, improve your ability to concentrate, and help you to relax.

Music to Concentrate By

There is one other method you can use to help yourself to relax and it requires no conscious effort on your part. Studies done in Eastern Europe and more recently in this country have found that certain pieces of baroque music can improve your concentration and memory while helping you to relax. Specifically the baroque music that has the greatest impact is the *largo* movements that are played at approximately one beat per second. Although it is not recommended that this music be used to replace the other relaxation methods you've learned, the music can be used to maintain a relaxed state during reading or study sessions. If you'd like to acquire recordings using this music, here are a few of the composers and titles that have proven to be effective: Bach's largo movement from Concerto in G Minor for Flute and Strings, Handel's largo movement from Concerto no. 1 in F from "Music for the Royal Fireworks," and Vivaldi's largo movement from "Winter" from "The Four Seasons."

REPETITION

The final element in developing good concentration is the principle of repetition or practice. The most important way repetition benefits concentration is that by repeating the basics of any skill certain aspects become subconscious or automatic. This allows you to place more of your mind's attention on the desired outcome and less on the mechanics of what you're doing.

Think back to when you were first learning how to drive a car. Do you remember how you had to put your attention on every little detail? You were conscious of how you held the steering wheel, how hard you pressed the gas pedal and the brake. To top it off, you were not yet used to the various rules of traffic. Consequently, you placed much of your attention on the mechanics of driving as opposed to the objective of driving, and chances are that you were not the best driver at that time. However, since then, certain elements through repetition have become second nature. Today, you quite likely hit the brake pedal automatically when you come to a stoplight, or the gas pedal at a green light. You're a better driver today because repetition allows you to place less attention on the mechanics of driving and more on safely reaching your destination.

Repetition has always been the most important factor in achieving peak performance in any field. In one sense, it seems reasonable that gifted individuals, who have a particular aptitude for a skill, shouldn't have to practice as much as other people. But that's not the case. Just the opposite is true. The best in every field, whether they be musicians, artists, or tennis players, practice more, not less, and that's how they get to be the best. Olympic gymnasts practice up to eight hours a day for years to make a performance seem effortless. Through repetition, the basics become second nature, so when it comes time to perform, these individuals can then concentrate on their objective.

Points to Remember

The AAIRR formula: **A**ttitude, **A**ttention, **I**nterest, **Re**laxation, and **R**epetition. All of these elements must be present simultaneously for good concentration.

Attitude:

1. Keep your mind on what you want.
2. Use positive words, pictures, and emotions.
3. Relax, and then use repetition on a daily basis to imprint positive affirmations and pictures on your subconscious mind.

Attention:

1. Eliminate external distractions:
    a. Create the proper work environment.
    b. Read with little or no noise or one-beat-per-second baroque music.
    c. Organize your work space and have the proper tools.
2. Eliminate internal distractions:
    a. Relax
    b. Know your internal body clock.
    c. Verbalize and visualize what you want.

d. Set specific, realistic goals.

e. Separate your goals into manageable sections.

Interest:

1. Interest is fuel for concentration.

2. If possible, choose areas to concentrate where you have a natural interest.

3. When interest isn't present, replace interest with motivation and ask yourself, "What would motivate me to keep my mind on this project?"

Relaxation:

Relaxation frees the mind to put more energy and attention on the task at hand and less attention on the physical body.

Relaxation Exercises

1. Deep Breathing

    a. Sit comfortably with your arms at your sides.

    b. Using your diaphragm, inhale slowly through your nose for a count of four.

    c. Hold your breath for a count of four.

    d. Rest for a count of four.

    e. Repeat the exercise two more times, each time adding an additional count of two to each step.

2. Melting Snowman Exercise

    a. Using the deep-breathing exercise from above, mentally count backward from fifty to zero while visualizing a snowman gradually melting.

    b. Keep the picture as clear and as vivid as you can.

    c. Note when the picture fades.

    d. To improve concentration, set subgoals to maintain a clear image of a gradually melting snowman for an additional five counts each time.

Repetition:

1. Repetition allows certain elements of any skill to become subconscious or automatic, thus freeing the mind to place greater focus on the desired outcome.

2. Practice can be either mental, through the use of visualization or mental rehearsal, or physical. However, when possible, the best approach is to use a combination of both techniques.

CHAPTER 10

COMPREHENSION

Questions to keep in mind: What is comprehension? Is comprehension objective? Are there different types of comprehension?

A synonym for comprehension is *understanding*, but what does the term really mean? After all, there are many different levels of understanding. For example, let's assume you read a movie review before you see the movie. You believe your comprehension to be good; you fully understand whether or not the critic liked the movie and for what reasons. Then you actually go to see the movie, afterwards rereading the review. Is your comprehension the same? No, it's different because you have more information. It's a deeper, richer type of understanding, but the review itself has not changed. So what has changed? You have changed. Therefore, comprehension is not a constant; it changes as you change.

FACTORS TO IMPROVE COMPREHENSION

You can improve comprehension by understanding what affects it. One important factor was discussed in the last chapter—focus your attention, and comprehension is almost certain to improve. However, good concentration does not guarantee good comprehension.

Three additional factors contribute greatly to your overall ability to comprehend.

1. ELIMINATION OF LEARNING BARRIERS

To obtain your best comprehension, you need to remove all psychological learning barriers that you or someone else may have imprinted on your mind. You need to accept as fact that you are capable of learning and understanding anything. You may be thinking, "Well, if I can learn anything, then why haven't I?" There may be reasons, but none of them have anything to do with your real ability to learn. Perhaps you had an instructor who wasn't a good communicator or didn't really understand the subject well himself; maybe you had a poorly written textbook; or possibly you simply did not pay attention in class. However, none of these reasons has anything to do with your true ability to learn. You need to remove these negative learning barriers by overriding them with daily repetition of positive words, pictures, and emotions while in a physically relaxed state.

Exercise to Eliminate Learning Barriers

To create a conducive mind-set for good comprehension:

- Relax your body.
- Repeat two or three positive affirmations, such as *I can learn anything; I have excellent comprehension.*
- Picture in detail the benefits of your verbal affirmations.
- Repeat twice daily.

2. BACKGROUND KNOWLEDGE

Background knowledge is probably the single most important factor in determining your comprehension. It's the knowledge that you bring to the subject, and it includes vocabulary as well as related ideas. For example, let's assume as a freshman in college you have registered for an introductory course in economics; then you decide to make economics your major. After graduation four years later, reread your introductory economics book and you are likely to have much better comprehension—but not because you are any more intelligent. You simply have acquired more background knowledge. Much of the terminology by this time would be familiar, as would many of the basic concepts. The more background knowledge you have in a given area, the better your comprehension will be.

Building a knowledge base for good comprehension is similar to building a house. In order for your house to be sturdy and structurally sound, you start with a good plan or blueprints, a solid foundation, and quality materials, and then build from there. If you start with faulty plans or use cheap materials, or have a weak foundation, chances are that no matter how well built the rest of the house is, at some point the house is going to start to collapse. Comprehension works in exactly the same way. For example, if you attempt to learn calculus before you master algebra or trigonometry, you're attempting to build comprehension on a weak foundation.

Building Background Knowledge

The best readers are usually people who read the most. Why? They acquire the most background knowledge, which gives them better comprehension, making reading more enjoyable. Conversely, people who don't read much or dislike reading will find it difficult to build sufficient background knowledge, so that, when they *do* read, their comprehension cannot be at the highest level.

One of the keys to improving comprehension is to build a strong knowledge base for the subject that you are covering. By using effective speed reading, you can return to any subject that you may have had trouble with in the past or move into an entirely new area and build background knowledge fast.

You can build strong comprehension in any area by using the following approach. Let's assume that you presently have difficulty comprehending material in the general sciences such as biology, physics, and chemistry because you never really grasped the fundamentals. Here's what you can do to build the necessary background knowledge for good comprehension:

- Go to your local library and check out early grade school science books from the fourth grade on and begin to put your speed reading skills to work.
- Quickly read through these early books to acquire a solid foundation, and then progressively move on to junior high and high school texts, and finally college-level textbooks.
- Read current material in the same subject matter and make note of whether your comprehension has improved significantly.

Using the Structure of the Book

You can dramatically improve your comprehension by simply paying attention to the structure of the book and using it to your advantage. Little things can make a big difference in helping your comprehension. For example, read the front and back covers, the inside jacket, and any information about the author. This takes a couple of minutes or less, but it often gives you the main point of the book as well as the author's background, expertise, and point of view. Here are some other easy tips in using the structure of the book to improve comprehension:

- Read over the table of contents. Chapter titles are main ideas and also give you the progression of ideas and thoughts. If you already have background in this area, you'll be able to see if the book repeats information you already have or contains new information.
- Read introductions and conclusions. An introduction usually states the author's main objective in writing

the book, and the conclusion summarizes the book's main points.

- Spend a minute or two surveying the index or glossary to recognize familiar or unfamiliar terminology so that you can determine how much background you already have and how much time you're likely to spend learning new vocabulary.

3. PURPOSE

If you do the above exercise with a subject that gave you problems in the past, almost assuredly the material will now seem easier. Why? The reason is due to the third element for good comprehension, which is a well-defined need or purpose for reading the material. Chances are that when you first encountered this subject, you lacked the motivation or interest necessary for good comprehension. Interest or motivation is a necessary ingredient for good concentration, which directly impacts your comprehension. Perhaps you now see a real need or purpose for this information. Maybe this knowledge will lead to a better job in today's marketplace or allow you to graduate with an advanced degree. With motivation and speed reading, you can catch up with and even pass the competition as your background knowledge continues to build.

Points to Remember

1. Comprehension means understanding.
2. There are many different levels of understanding.
3. Comprehension changes as you change.
4. Elements of good comprehension:
  a. Concentration (use the AAIRR formula).
  b. Eliminate learning barriers by overriding them with positive words, pictures, and emotions while in a relaxed state.
  c. A well-defined need or purpose gives you motivation.

CHAPTER 11

DEVELOP A SUPER MEMORY

Memory Quiz: Read the following list once and then on a sheet of paper write down as many items as you can recall in order: book, telephone, sandwich, Humphrey Bogart, refrigerator, tree, computer, bathtub, tennis, eyeglasses, dog, supervisor, bowling ball

What are you most likely to remember and why? What factors naturally improve or hinder your ability to remember? The answers to these questions will be the basis for the powerful memory systems that you are about to learn, so that you will be able to remember almost anything quickly, without the need for tedious repetition. But first a little background on the physiology and psychology of memory.

THE PHYSIOLOGY OF MEMORY

The average adult brain weighs less than three pounds, yet it can store more information than all the libraries in the world. It contains between ten billion and a hundred billion neurons that communicate with one another through electrical and chemical messages. The total number of connections between the brain's neurons is astronomical and is estimated to be greater than ten to the fifteenth power.

Memories are transmitted by tiny gaps between the nerve cells called synapses. In essence, the synapse is like a bridge between two brain cells that allows information to pass from one cell to the next. There are over ten trillion synapses in the average brain and they connect your brain cells in an intricate network. The brain cells relay information through electrical impulses which some neuroscientists theorize cause chemical changes that are then encoded as memories.

In order for your brain to work at peak efficiency for both memory and concentration, certain vital nutrients are necessary on a daily basis. Here is a chart that summarizes the latest research on nutrition and memory:

What You Need	Where It's Found	What It Does
choline	lecithin, most meats, soybeans	improves memory
vitamin B_{12}	dairy products, fish, meat	deficiency impairs memory and concentration
vitamin B_1 (thiamin)	wheat germ, green leafy vegetables, lean meats	needed for good memory
vitamin B_6	brewer's yeast, bananas, peanuts, poultry	needed for concentration
vitamin B_3 (niacin)	fish, brewer's yeast, beans, peanuts, poultry	needed for concentration
vitamin C	citrus fruits, tomatoes, broccoli, green peppers	removes toxins; reduces stress; helps concentration
calcium	dairy products, green leafy vegetables	deficiency impairs memory
physical exercise	running, jogging, walking, swimming	reduces stress; improves memory by increasing oxygen flow to brain
relaxation exercise	deep breathing	reduces stress; increases oxygen flow to brain; improves concentration

THE PSYCHOLOGY OF MEMORY

The Ebbinghaus Experiments

Some of the first and most important work conducted on the psychological components of short-term and long-term memory was done by Hermann Ebbinghaus in the late nineteenth century. Briefly here's what Ebbinghaus found out:

1. In memorizing lists, people remembered more items from the beginning and ending and less of what fell in the middle. This is known as the *primacy and recency effect.*
2. The majority of forgetting occurs almost immediately after learning, and as much as 70 percent of the information is lost within 24 hours unless an immediate review is done. You will learn more about this in the next chapter when you read about the RWAP study system.
3. If a large amount of information needs to be learned, memory improves when the material is divided into equal parts, no more than forty minutes allowed for each, and when short breaks of approximately five minutes are taken between each new section.
4. A brief review of previously learned information improves memory in learning new information.

Space Aliens Invade Earth: the Von Restorff Effect

Another important psychological discovery in the way our natural memories work was made by a psychologist by the name of Von Restorff. He found that we remember outstanding items in lists of similar items. Perhaps the best way to see this principle in action is to think back on your own life. Do you have a conscious recollection of every single day of your life or even every day for the last two months? Almost certainly, your answer is no. Most of the days probably run together so that you really can't discern one day from the next. The reason for this is that, for the most part, they were very much alike. However, if you think back now to those days that you do remember vividly, there is probably something unique that makes them stand out from the rest—perhaps a promotion, a birthday, an anniversary, college graduation, or prom night. The point is that the days you do remember vividly are different, somehow out of the ordinary. We remember the unusual, not the ordinary. In fact, do you remember the subtitle to this section or even the actor's name in the Memory Quiz you took at the beginning of the chapter? If you do, perhaps it's because of the Von Restorff Effect.

THE MAGIC NUMBER SEVEN

Another significant discovery in the field of memory came from a psychologist by the name of George Miller. Miller found that short-term (left brain) memory is limited to approximately seven units of thought plus or minus two. Miller wrote about this phenomenon in his renowned paper "The Magic Number Seven Plus or Minus Two." In fact, if you have ever wondered why telephone numbers use only seven digits, it's that people had a difficult time remembering, when numbers contained more than seven digits.

The Magic Number Seven is also relevant to recall and comprehension. In reading a long sentence, you may forget what was at the beginning of the sentence by the time you get to the end, because you were required to keep more than seven words in your short-term memory. It's important to understand that the Magic Number Seven refers to units and not items, so if you can group more items into a unit, you can remember far more items than seven. For example, a social security number contains nine digits, but it's divided into three units. Similarly, speed readers may take a line that's fifteen words, and divide it into three five-word units. By increasing the size of each unit, you stay well within the Magic Number Seven Plus or Minus Two.

The Magic Number Seven applies only to your short-term left-brain memory. The right hemisphere of your brain does not have this limitation. In fact, your right brain has an infinite capacity both to create and to recognize pictures. In one classic study, subjects were shown over ten thousand photographs and there was a recognition factor of more than 99 percent. Thus, if you are to go beyond the Magic Number Seven, you must learn to: 1) increase the size of each unit so that it contains more information; 2) convert left-brain abstracts into concrete right-brain images. Both of these achievements are accomplished with the memory systems you will learn about shortly.

ORGANIZATION

The more organized that information is as it enters your mind, the greater the likelihood is that you will remember that information. Without organization, information becomes chaos to the mind, and your mind will discard the information. One of the benefits of using a Slash Memory Tree to take notes is that it makes you organize the information as you write it down. The Slash Memory Tree is an example of a *mnemonic-organized base*.

What is a mnemonic-organized base? First, mnemonics is a technique that helps you improve your memory. Almost assuredly you have used mnemonics before. For example, *Every good boy does fine* is a mnemonic device to help you learn the notes on a music staff; *I before e except after c* is a mnemonic rhyme to help you remember that rule of spelling; and *Thirty days hath September, April, June, and November* is a mnemonic device to help you remember how many days are in each month.

The Greeks and Romans over two thousand years ago were the first to introduce mnemonic systems that allowed them to recall large amounts of information without the need for constant repetition.

A mnemonic-organized base combines mnemonics with the principle of organization. Any familiar organized structure can be used as the base, such as numbers, the alphabet, or a room in your home. You will learn more about this shortly.

ASSOCIATION

All memory, to a certain degree, is dependent on the principle of association. Everything in your mind has to be connected to some other information; otherwise your mind will discard it. Another way of saying this is that in order for you to learn something new, you must connect it with something you already know. In essence, the data already recorded are like hooks where you can hang new information and that information in turn can hold other information and it goes on and on this way. So there is never any danger that your memory will somehow fill up. It's just the opposite: the more you know, the more you can know.

Association is also a triggering process. For example, what is the date of your birthday? Immediately a specific date comes to the forefront of your mind. Now, you probably were not thinking of that date until the question was asked. The question triggered the data instantaneously from somewhere in your memory bank.

Another interesting characteristic of associations is that they can be connected in many different ways. Take the word *family* and think of some of the associations you have connected to this word. You might think of parents, brothers, sisters, aunts, uncles, cousins, grandparents. All of these may be connected to the association of family. In fact, one item can literally have hundreds, even thousands of separate associations. For instance, a cousin of yours might certainly be associated with the concept of family, but that same cousin might also be thought of as a friend or possibly someone you dislike, or in connection with a certain profession, a particular place, and on and on. You have a network of associations that can cross over in staggering numbers.

Associations can come from any of our five senses. For example, a certain smell, such as a cologne or perfume, will bring back memories of someone you used to date or be friends with. Sounds are another way associations are triggered. An "oldie but goodie" comes on the radio and immediately you think back to where you were, whom you were with, how you felt at the time you first heard the song. All nostalgia is related to our associations.

The associations just mentioned happen naturally. You don't try to force them to come into being—they simply do. However, there are certain elements that will tend to make associations stronger and more vivid, thus more likely to be remembered.

1. The Unusual

We remember things that are different, even bizarre. Remember our friend Von Restorff. It's back to space aliens and Humphrey Bogart. The first rule of associations is that they will be much more likely to be recalled if they are unusual or out of the ordinary; the more absurd the association, the better.

2. Visual, Concrete, and Vivid

It's easier to remember visual associations than verbal or abstract ones. In fact, every association you make from this point on should be vivid enough so that you can make a mental picture of the items you want to memorize, and you must visualize them in some unusual way. Below you will find ways to make your associations conform to these guidelines:

- Use out-of-proportion size or quantities.
- Use vivid colors.
- Use 3-D imagery.
- Have inanimate objects take on human characteristics.
- Use humor.

- Use action.
- Use all five senses.

Association Practice Exercises

Let's practice linking items together using the above criteria. First, think back to the Memory Quiz at the beginning of this chapter. How many of those items can you still recall? Take a minute to write down as many items as you can in order. Chances are you recalled only a few, possibly one or two from the beginning and ending of the list (primacy and recency) and possibly Humphrey Bogart (the Von Restorff Effect). But now you are going to memorize each of these items by linking them together with absurd visual imagery. Not only will you have to go over the list just once, but you will also memorize the list frontward and backward, and you'll recall it even days later. Here's how you do it. You must link items in pairs in a continuous chain. Using the words in the memory quiz, do your best to make clear images of the following. Visualize a giant *book* talking on the *telephone;* the *telephone* is extremely hungry and is eating a *sandwich* with *Humphrey Bogart* in between two pieces of bread, while *Bogart* holds up a *refrigerator* with his free hand. The refrigerator door explodes and out shoots a giant shivering *tree* with thousands of glowing *computers* (perhaps Apple computers) growing and ripening on its branches. Some ripe *computers* (glowing dark green) fall and are caught by an athletic *bathtub* that is right in the middle of a crucial point in its *tennis* match with a pair of nearsighted *eyeglasses*. Suddenly, on a double fault the *eyeglasses* shatter, as a giant *dog* crashes through, walking your least-liked *supervisor* on a leash with a *bowling ball* stuck in his mouth.

Obviously, associations are better when you make them yourself, but this example gives you the general idea. No matter how ridiculous the story seems, if you made the pictures, the information is recalled. Test it for yourself. In fact, there's a very good chance you memorized the list backward as well as forward. Write as many words in order as you can recall frontward and then backward.

MNEMONIC-ORGANIZED BASES

Mnemonic-organized bases can be used to create powerful memory systems. Not every system will work as well for you, but you should experiment with them all. All good mnemonic-organized bases have the following in common: 1) they use what you already know to learn something new (i.e., numbers, the alphabet, or a familiar room); 2) they require that you make unusual, vivid associations between the organized base and the items you want to remember.

THE ALPHABET SYSTEM

Applications. To memorize any kind of list, appointments, main ideas from readings, speeches, and presentations.

Organized Base. All 26 letters of the English alphabet.

Objective. To convert the letters of the alphabet into concrete visual peg words and then use these to link with the information that you want to remember.

Basics. Choose standard concrete peg words that begin with each letter of the alphabet. Below are examples of possible peg words. Feel free to make up your own list, but the key is to keep the peg words you choose consistent each time you use the system. Then link your alphabet peg words with the information you want to memorize.

A apple	D dog
B book	E eagle
C cat	F fence

G gardener
H heart
I Indian
J jelly
K king
L light bulb
M monkey
N nose
O ostrich
P pencil

Q queen
R race car
S snake
T ticket
U umbrella
V van
W witch
X xylophone
Y yolk
Z zebra

Exercise. To improve your vocabulary, use the Alphabet Memory System to memorize the common prefixes and suffixes listed in the following chart.

Examples. The first alphabet peg word is your "A" word *apple*, so you must connect apple with the first prefix *un-*. *Un-* means *not*, such as in *unreliable*, which means *not reliable*. So perhaps you visualize an *unreliable apple* that doesn't show up in your fruit bowl. Let's go to the second prefix *ab-*, which also means *not*, such as in the word *abnormal*, which means *not normal*. You must link this with the second alphabet peg word, *book*. Picture an *abnormal book*; perhaps you'll visualize a giant bright red book that doesn't have any pages or has only blank pages.

Prefix	Meaning	Example	Suffix	Meaning	Example
un-	not	unreliable	-less	without	hopeless
ab-	away from	abnormal	-y	inclined to	sleepy
di-	to separate	divide	-ar, -er, -or	one who	actor, painter
re-	back	recall	-ness	state of	carelessness
ex-	out of	exclude	-able	able to do	capable
pro-	in favor of	promote	-acy	state of	accuracy
im-	not	immature	-age	state of	breakage
ad-	toward	advertise	-arium	place for	aquarium
bi-	two	bicycle	-ary	place for	dictionary
pre-	before	preschool	-hood	state of	childhood
dis-	take away	dispose	-tude	state of	attitude
hypo-	under	hypochondria	-cule	very small	molecule

Prefix	Meaning	Example	Suffix	Meaning	Example
macro-	large	macrocosm	-ist	one who	terrorist
fin-	end	finish	-oid	resemble	tabloid
auto-	self	automatic	-meter	measure	thermometer
arch-	chief	archbishop	-ade	result of	decade
bene-	good	benefit	-ize	to make	publicize
com-	together	companion	-ion	condition of	persuasion
contra-	against	contradict	-ic	relating to	historic
hemi-	half	hemisphere	-ine	a compound	chlorine
il-	not	illogical	-ment	result of	resentment
inter-	beween	interstate	-al	relating to	sensual
out-	beyond	outstanding	-ful	full of	graceful
para-	beyond	paranormal	-fy, -ify	make	satisfy
post-	after	postdate	-cise	to cut	precise
sub-	under	submarine	-sis	condition of	hypnosis
tele-	far	telescope			
eu-	pleasant	eulogy			
hyper-	over	hyperactive			
de-	away from	defend			
trans-	across	transaction			
en-	into	enroll			

THE ROOM SYSTEM

Applications. To memorize lists of any kind, main ideas from readings, speeches or presentations, facts, appointments. Also, to separate and categorize large bodies of information.

Organized Base. Any familiar room or organized structure (i.e., bedroom, conference room, office, baseball field, game board, characters on favorite television show).

Objective. To link information you want to memorize to objects already in a familiar room or structure.

Basics. Choose a starting point in any familiar room or organized structure. Then, move clockwise connecting concrete objects already in the room or structure with the new information you need to remember.

The Room System is one of the easiest memory systems to apply and is actually one of the oldest. A variation on the Room System dates back to the Romans and Greeks over two thousand years ago. One of the great advantages of the Room System is that you can apply it immediately after learning it. You are going to use information you already know, but in a new, creative, and fun way. The Room System is also extremely flexible since you can choose one room, a number of rooms, or any other organized structure such as a game board, a baseball diamond, or even a favorite television show.

Let's run through a brief example of how you might use the Room System. Think of your bedroom right now. Visualize all the items already in the room: your dresser, a night table with a lamp, your dirty clothes, a painting, a desk, a stack of magazines, a clock radio, a television, a telephone, and so on. Every item in your room is a potential hook to hang new information on. For this example, let's assume you are taking a course in economics. Your bed will be the starting point in the room, and the first term you want to memorize is *Gross National Product*. Visualize yourself pulling back the covers of your bed and finding underneath every imaginable variety of goods and services. You see factories, people selling hotdogs, doctors, construction workers, farmers, auto showrooms, etc. Replace the covers. Move clockwise in your room and perhaps you come to a basket of dirty laundry. The next concept you want to remember is *supply and demand*, so since there is very little demand for your dirty clothes, your supply is great. Picture dirty clothes piled to the ceiling! Suddenly, the marketplace changes and dirty clothes are in great demand; you now will visualize your supply of dirty clothes shrinking. For as many terms and definitions as you have to learn and memorize, continue to move clockwise in your room and associate concrete items already there (things you already know) to the new information in an absurd way.

The Room System is extremely flexible and allows you to put different subject matter in separate rooms. So your marketing proposal might be in your living room while your budget report is associated with items in your kitchen. Instead of a room, you can use any organized structure that you are familiar with. Use your favorite soap opera, a baseball field, or even a Monopoly game board as your organized base. Even the human body can be used as an organized base: your head, eyes, ears, mouth, fingers, etc.

Points to Remember

1. The human brain contains between ten billion and a hundred billion neurons, which are set at birth.
2. Memories are transmitted by synapses, which act as bridges between the brain cells. There are over ten trillion synapses in the average human brain.
3. You are more likely to remember items that fall at the beginning and end of a particular sequence and more likely to forget what falls in the middle.
4. Memory declines quickly after learning, but an immediate review of the material can save much of the information from being forgotten.
5. Memory improves if you divide large learning assignments into equal parts of no more than forty minutes and then separate them by short breaks.
6. A brief review of information learned previously will improve memory when learning new information.
7. In lists of similar items we are more likely to recall unusual or outstanding items.
8. The capacity of short-term, left-brain memory is seven units plus or minus two; however, if you increase the size of each unit you can recall much more information.
9. Your right-brain memory has no such limitations and can recall an infinite number of pictures or images.

10. Association is a connecting or triggering process. Everything you have stored in your brain acts as hooks to learn new information.

11. Organization allows you to file and retrieve information from your mind.

12. A mnemonic-organized base combines association and organization to form powerful memory systems such as the Alphabet and Room Systems.

CHAPTER 12

THE RWAP STUDY SYSTEM

Directions: You can determine both your reading speed and your comprehension for this chapter. Read for your best comprehension. When you finish, record your reading time estimated to the nearest quarter minute and then go on to answer the questions.

—BEGIN TIMING

Have you ever had a lesson on how to master difficult or technical reading? If your answer is no, you are not alone. Most people have never had a lesson on how to study or how to best approach difficult reading at any time during their academic years. The majority develop their own methods that are often inadequate and inefficient. This is unfortunate since the ability to study effectively increases the chances of success in school, business, and most other professions. But it's not too late. Individuals with a desire to learn the proper study techniques can improve their productivity and expertise.

The RWAP Study System (pronounced "rap") stands for "*R*epetition *W*ith *A* *P*urpose." The basic premise of the system is that in order to master difficult or detailed reading, you need to review the material more than once. Many people make the mistake of assuming they have to comprehend and recall everything the first time through the material. Not only is this unrealistic, but it is usually far more time-consuming in the long run. The RWAP system acknowledges the likelihood that you probably will not understand everything in only one reading. It approaches the material systematically with each repetition having a distinct purpose.

The RWAP system approaches technical reading in the same way that you might approach a 5000-piece jigsaw puzzle. If you were to begin assembling a puzzle of this size, where would you start? An experienced puzzler will most likely begin with the frame or border pieces because these are the easiest to fit together, and more importantly, all the other pieces in the puzzle must fit somewhere between the borders. After you finish the frame, you'd move on to the sections that you can easily put together because of distinct patterns, shapes, colors, etc.

And what pieces would you save for last? The answer is: the most difficult pieces. Now that you have the frame and the other sections in place, it's easier to see where the difficult pieces fit into place. So let's see how the RWAP Study System utilizes this same principle.

STEP 1—THE OVERVIEW

The overview is the frame of your puzzle. It gives you the big picture of the material you are about to read. Its purpose is to give you a sense of the whole and to see how the material breaks down structurally. To get an overview of a book, read the following: the front and back covers, the table of contents, information about the author, the preface, introduction, and conclusion. This should give you a general sense of content and the author's point of view.

Next, move through the material quickly using the Horseshoe or Question Mark Hand Motion to observe the book's structure. Ask yourself: Does your book have a subtitle, subheads, pictures, photographs, graphs, charts, chapter summaries, questions, a glossary, italicized areas, or any other structural elements of importance? Please note that the purpose of the overview *is not* to acquire specific information about these areas. You simply want to determine whether they exist. Once you know the author's road map, you can use this information to plan the most effective strategy to meet your reading purpose.

STEP 2–DETERMINE YOUR PURPOSE

You must now determine exactly why you are reading the material and what you need to get out of it. Remember, in order for a goal to be effective it must be extremely specific. Are you reading the material for a detailed presentation, an exam, background knowledge, or for some other purpose? But let's go one step further. Let's assume that you are reading a textbook for an exam. That's still far too general. What type of exam is being given? For instance, an essay test requires far more detail than a multiple-choice exam. Also, you need to know whether your instructor tests predominantly from the book or from lectures, and if it's a combination of the two, what percentage is designated to each. All of this information is necessary to help you effectively reach your reading goal. Purpose brings into play book control and active reading. Tell your mind exactly what you want and it will go into the material and find it for you.

STEP 3–MANAGEABLE SECTIONS

Once you have established your purpose for reading the material, divide the assignment into manageable sections. In this context, manageable means nonthreatening to the mind. You will use realistic subgoals to reach your overall goal of completing the reading. When possible, work from subhead to subhead. A subhead is a small unit, but it contains information about one main idea within its boundaries. If your book does not use subheads, divide the chapter into three- to five-page manageable sections. At any point, you can expand or reduce your sections. The key is to make each section manageable for you.

Follow this procedure for each manageable section: 1) Block off only one manageable section at a time by using two paper clips; 2) Work exclusively in that one small part, telling yourself that this is all you have to read for the time being; 3) When you finish, allow yourself a short break as a reward; 4) Now mark off your next manageable section; 5) Repeat the entire procedure until you have completed the assignment. By working with manageable sections you will receive three distinct benefits.

Manageable Sections Get You Started

Have you ever looked at a lengthy work assignment or a major research project and become psychologically fatigued before you start? This fatigue usually results in procrastination. You may find yourself looking for all kinds of distractions to keep from starting. You have to sharpen your pencils, you have to make just one or two telephone calls, or you have to make one more trip to the water cooler. Before you know it you've decided that you'll just start tomorrow. The problem is that your mind has focused on the whole assignment. You feel overwhelmed by how much needs to be done.

Manageable sections eliminate procrastination and are essential for all long-term goals. They reduce the initial hesitation of starting. Starting is the hardest part of any project. However, once you begin and build some momentum, it's much easier to move toward the completion of your goal.

Manageable Sections Improve Performance

Concentration and motivation levels increase when your goal is within reach. For example, a marathon runner who is drained and physically exhausted somehow musters enough extra energy to sprint when the finish line comes into view. Most people in our society are conditioned to work toward finish lines. When you use manageable sections, each ending paper clip becomes a finish line. Consequently, your concentration and performance will increase throughout the chapter as opposed to only the one time this would naturally occur.

Manageable Sections Improve Recall

In the last chapter, you learned of the phenomenon known as the *primacy and recency effect*. In short, people are more likely to remember information that appears at the beginning (primacy) and at the end (recency) of a particular sequence, and most likely to forget information that falls in the middle. Unfortunately, in lengthy journal articles, most of the information falls in the middle. Consequently, even if you had excellent comprehension, there is still a very good chance that you would not recall the majority of the material.

However, when you divide the article into manageable sections, you create many beginnings and endings and reduce the middle areas. Consequently, your overall recall of the material improves.

Take a short break of approximately five minutes at the completion of each manageable section. A short break will serve two functions. First, a break is an incentive to finish, and second, a short break will create the necessary beginnings and endings that will improve your memory.

STEP 4–PRE-READ FOR MAIN IDEAS

The purpose of the pre-read is to locate the main ideas in the material so that you can use them to create attention and interest during the actual reading. In our jigsaw puzzle example, the pre-read is finding the easy pieces to put together. There are two parts to the pre-read: general and specific.

General Pre-read

The general pre-read focuses on finding the main ideas from the chapter as a whole. From the overview, you know whether there is a summary, a conclusion, or questions at the end of the chapter. If any of these exist, you should read them first. Why is this so important? Here's a real-life illustration. At Harvard, the Bureau of Study Council gave a group of incoming freshmen thirty pages of detailed reading. The students were told that an hour exam would be given to them on the material in a week, but twenty-two minutes later they were told to stop reading and asked to discuss what they had read. Although a good number of students could recall detailed information about the reading, when they were asked to write a short summary of the chapter only fifteen out of the fifteen hundred who took the test could do so. These fifteen students were the only ones who had looked ahead and read the summary before starting to read the chapter.

Specific Pre-read

The purpose of the specific pre-read is to locate main ideas, but it is restricted to one manageable section. The specific pre-read is fast. Using your hand as a pacer, search for the main ideas in the most obvious places: subheads, italicized areas, graphs, charts, and the first and last line of each paragraph. When you finish, write in your own words the main points you are able to recall.

STEP 5–READ FOR DETAILS

When you complete the pre-read, you have enough information to focus your mind while you read. Use the main points you wrote down and turn them into mental questions. Read actively to fill in the details in order to meet your purpose. Do not linger over any difficult areas or take any notes at this point. Instead read to the end of each manageable section. Later, return to these troublesome areas and they are likely to seem easier since you'll have a better understanding of the whole.

Do not underscore what you consider to be important points during the initial reading. Instead, read with a pencil in hand and if you believe a point to be important, put a little check mark in the margin and continue on. By not underlining, you're less likely to lose your train of thought and you will ultimately save yourself countless hours of unnecessary study time. You really do not know how all the points fit together until you reach the end of the chapter, so you might underscore points at the beginning and middle of the chapter that are often not important. Good readers learn to discriminate between essential and nonessential information. William James once said, "The essence of genius is knowing what to overlook." Putting check marks in the margin will help you to accomplish this objective.

STEP 6—SUMMARIZE IN YOUR OWN WORDS

After reading each manageable section, take time to summarize in your own words the main ideas. It is best to write your summary on a sheet of paper, as the physical act of writing helps you to retain the information. A Slash Memory Tree is recommended. When you can rephrase information in your own words, it shows that you understand the concepts being presented. This will help you to crystallize and to retain what you have learned, as well as make you aware of those areas where you still need to focus.

Another positive effect of summarizing in your own words deals with the correlation of time to the rate of forgetting. As discussed in the chapter on memory, the majority of forgetting occurs immediately after learning. Therefore, an immediate review in your own words after reading each manageable section will save a large percentage of that information from having to be relearned.

STEP 7–POST-READ

The post-read is a final check over the entire reading before moving on. The purpose of the post-read is to see how all the pieces fit together as a whole, to look for information you may have missed or that was unclear, and to read over the main points one last time. Do the post-read from the end of the reading to the beginning so that you will have a different perspective on the material. A different perspective is necessary in order to find the information that you may have missed. If you post-read the material from front to back, you might miss the same points that eluded you during the pre-read and reading.

The post-read is not another detailed reading. It is done selectively. Scan quickly over the material that you already understand or that is not important for your purpose. Then slow down to read the areas that you are unsure about or don't remember. The post-read is also the time to reread all of your check-marked areas. If you still find the material to be important, now is the time to underscore or take detailed notes.

STEP 8–REVIEW AT SPACED INTERVALS

In order to move the information from short-term to long-term memory, you must review the material at spaced intervals. The following system of review has been proven to be most effective.

Schedule	When to Review	Length of Review
First review	approximately 10 minutes after learning	5 to 10 minutes
Second review	within 24 hours after initial learning	5 minutes
Third review	approximately 1 week later	3 minutes
Fourth review	approximately 1 month later	3 minutes
Fifth review	approximately 6 months later	3 minutes

SUMMARY

Detailed learning requires that you go over the material more than once. The RWAP Study System is based on this premise and systematically has you repeat the information a minimum of four times: overview, pre-read, read, and post-read. Each repetition of the material has a distinct function as you move progressively from general information to specific details, until your purpose for reading the material has been met.
——STOP!

Record Reading Time (estimate to the nearest quarter minute) _____
Number of words in reading: 2400
To determine your reading rate, divide your reading time into the number of words in reading.

Test for Comprehension

Directions: For each of the following questions, circle the letter of the most correct answer.

1. RWAP stands for:
   a. Read With A Purpose
   b. Retention With A Purpose
   c. Review With A Purpose
   d. Repetition With A Purpose

2. The purpose of the overview is:
   a. to get a sense of the whole
   b. to locate specific details about the reading
   c. to become familiar with the book's structure
   d. both a and c

3. The reading test given to Harvard freshmen illustrates that:
   a. reading the summary first is not helpful

    b. reading the summary first allows you to make sense of the details

    c. reading the summary first is only a good idea if you are tested immediately

    d. both a and c

4. The purpose of the pre-read is to:
    a. locate main ideas
    b. locate information you may have missed
    c. locate detailed information
    d. obtain structural information about the book

5. Summarizing in your own words after each manageable section *does not:*
    a. affect your memory
    b. define your purpose
    c. crystallize and imprint what you have learned
    d. make you aware of areas you still need to work on

6. According to studies in psychology, people are more likely to recall information:
    a. at the end
    b. at the beginning
    c. in the middle
    d. both a and b

7. The post-read:
    a. is the time to underscore nonessential information
    b. is another detailed reading
    c. helps you to locate information you may have missed
    d. focuses primarily on locating main ideas

8. Which of the following is not a benefit of manageable sections?
    a. improved performance
    b. improved memory

    c. getting started
    d. none of the above

9. The statement "If you know what you're looking for, you have a better chance of finding it" refers to:
    a. summarizing in your own words
    b. determining your purpose
    c. working in manageable sections
    d. reviewing at spaced intervals

<u>Directions:</u> For the following questions, write T for true and F for false.

10. Main ideas can be found in subheads. _____

11. Never move on until you fully understand all difficult sections. _____

12. Manageable sections are usually one complete chapter. _____

13. The majority of forgetting occurs immediately after learning. _____

14. Subgoals are unrealistic measures of progress. _____

15. Taking notes and underscoring while you read are the most effective ways to assure that you only study the important points. _____

<u>Directions:</u> Fill in the blanks with the appropriate answers.

16. Reading the summary, conclusion, and questions at the end of the chapter is called a _____ pre-read.

17. You should post-read from the _____ of the chapter to the _____ to get a different perspective on the material.

18. You should _____ at spaced intervals to retain as much information as possible.

19. Determining your purpose for a reading assignment gives your mind focus and improves _____ .

20. The best way to self-test yourself on the concepts being presented and reduce the amount of information you forget is to _____ after each manageable section.

Score: See the Key to check your answers. To arrive at your total score, multiply each correct answer by five. _____%

Answer Key

1. d	11. F
2. d	12. F
3. b	13. T
4. a	14. F
5. b	15. F
6. d	16. general
7. c	17. back to front, end to beginning
8. d	18. review/take breaks
9. b	19. concentration
10. T	20. summarize in your own words

CHAPTER 13

HOW TO SPEED READ JUST ABOUT ANYTHING

Questions to keep in mind: What does an inverted pyramid style of writing mean? How does purpose affect the way you read business journals? How should you prioritize and categorize all business correspondence? Should you speed read all your reading?

You can speed read practically anything by combining the speed reading techniques you've learned along with various elements of the RWAP Study System. Different types of material require different approaches. In this chapter, you'll learn speed reading strategies for newspapers, magazines, business correspondences, and novels.

NEWSPAPERS

When reading a daily newspaper, begin by overviewing and pre-reading the main stories of the day. Many newspapers have designed their layout to help you do just that. For example, the front page of *The Wall Street Journal* has a summary of the main stories of the day on business and finance as well as worldwide news. By reading this first, you have an overview of the most important news and the section and page where you can find more details about each story. Many newspapers provide a similar outline or summary approach of the day's top stories. Furthermore, each specific section of many newspapers has a brief summary of the main stories in slightly more detail. Take advantage of this valuable information and read through it quickly. Even if you don't read any further, you can gather most of the major news in just a few minutes of a good overview. If your newspaper does not provide an outline, read the boldfaced headlines on the first page of each section.

Newspapers are well designed for speed readers. They use narrow columns that allow you to easily read a whole line or two in a glance. Also, newspaper stories use an inverted pyramid style, in which the most essential information is always presented in the first few paragraphs while less important details are added later in the article.

Your purpose and interest should determine how much of the story you read past the first few paragraphs. For example, let's assume you are reading the sports section and there is a story about a baseball game. If you read the headline, and it says, "Home Team Wins Again" and that's all you care to know, then you need not read any further. However, if you're a big fan, you want to know who hit the winning run, who the losing pitcher was, how many errors were committed, etc. In other words, you need more detail than just who won the game. Perhaps you know one of the players and you want to specifically find out how he played; then you have to read for even more detail. If you happen to be a scout for an opposing team, you may read for even further detail. Purpose determines how much detail you need and, therefore, how much of the article you need to read.

MAGAZINES AND PROFESSIONAL JOURNALS

Magazines and professional journals require a somewhat different strategy than newspapers since they do not use an inverted pyramid style in their articles. Start by overviewing the magazine or journal by reading the front cover, which usually previews the primary story or stories. Turn then to the table of contents and read over the titles of the articles and any other information printed underneath. Next, prioritize the articles based on purpose and interest. For each article do the following:

1. Be as specific as possible in regard to what you want out of the material. Are you reading for your own personal knowledge or is it information that is necessary for your line of work?

2. Once you clearly define your purpose, pre-read the article for main ideas. Use this information to form mental questions to give your mind focus. Then read to meet your purpose.

3. Depending upon your purpose and the amount of detail you need, you may decide to post-read from back to front and take notes using the Slash Memory Tree.

BUSINESS MAIL

More than most types of reading, business mail and correspondence require the related skills of discrimination and flexibility. Unless you master these skills, you may find yourself playing a never-ending game of catch-up. Here are some tips to effectively handle incoming mail and correspondence:

1. Separate mail from known individuals or companies (A Mail) from those you do not recognize (B Mail).

2. Prioritize your A Mail in order of importance and urgency.

3. For each piece of mail do the following:
   a. Read the first paragraph or two.
   b. Quickly pre-read through the body of the letter.
   c. Read the last couple of paragraphs.
   d. On the basis of the above information, either read for more detail, discard, or delegate. Discipline yourself to make a decision the first time you handle each piece of mail.

4. After finishing the A Mail move on to your B Mail. Pre-reading is even more important when sorting through unsolicited mail. You can waste much of your day if you do not extract the intent of each letter quickly. Generally only about 20 percent of your B Mail is of any importance or interest, but that is still significant in regard to potential business opportunities. A quick, effective pre-read, as described in Step 3, will allow you to evaluate your B Mail in a minimal amount of time.

NOVELS

There is a great difference between reading a novel for relaxation as opposed to study. For example, if you were taking a course in Russian literature you might have to reproduce main ideas on exams, write a paper, or give an oral report. In this instance, you treat a novel like a textbook. Start with an overview by reading the front and back covers of the book, and information about the author. Determine your purpose: What do you need the material for? Then break the book into manageable sections. Pre-read each manageable section looking for main ideas, which in fiction means *characters*, *setting*, *major events*, and *mood*. Start a Slash Memory Tree with these four main topics on their own branches.

However, if you are reading for enjoyment, almost none of the above are necessary with the exception of a basic overview of the book's front and back cover and/or book jacket. This brief overview gives you enough information about the book's content to help focus your mind as you read.

To Speed Read or Not to Speed Read—A Flexible Skill

There are times when you may not want to speed read or when speed reading is inappropriate. For example, if you are reading to relax and you are on the couch or in bed, it's counterproductive to speed read or use your hand as a pacer. Your purpose is to slow the mind down, not speed it up.

Also, certain types of material do not lend themselves to speed reading. For example, you do not want to speed read poetry. Poetry is meant to be read and sounded out word by word. Some classic literature, such as works by Shakespeare, falls into this same category.

However, the advantage you have as a speed reader is that you have a choice of how fast you read different types of material. Average readers do not have this flexibility. They can only *walk* through their reading. You can *walk, jog, run*, and *sprint* when necessary. Speed reading is an extremely flexible skill that allows you to adjust your speed to meet your purpose. You can turn it on or turn it off, as you see fit.

CHAPTER 14 SUMMARY

Questions to keep in mind: What are the advantages of using the hand as a pacer? What is the mental game of speed reading? What are the two main principles of memory? What must you do to make speed reading a lifelong skill?

The objective of this book is to give you a wide variety of techniques to increase your reading speed and learning potential by effectively using your brain and body in tandem to achieve maximum results. Let's briefly review some of the main points one last time.

Most people's reading speeds are limited due to inadequate early training that never identified or corrected certain reading problems. The speed reading techniques in this book eliminate or reduce the following reading problems: word-by-word reading, poor concentration, subvocalization, unconscious regression, slow recovery time, and a weak vocabulary.

The cornerstone of these speed reading methods, the use of the hand as a pacer, has a number of advantages over other less effective speed reading approaches. The hand is a permanent and flexible reading machine. You vary the speed of your hand depending upon your purpose, the difficulty of the material, and your background knowledge.

Furthermore, the Speed Reading Hand Method helps you increase reading speed and comprehension in a number of ways. First, the hand gives your eyes a guide so they are less likely to lose their place and reread material. Similarly, the hand reduces the amount of time it takes your eyes to move from line to line. Also, using your hand as a pacer reduces the problem of subvocalization by directing your eyes across a line faster than you can silently pronounce every word. The hand makes it easier to both see and read groups of words with each fixation of your eyes. Finally, your hand adds rhythm to your reading, which activates and involves the right side of your brain.

Speed reading requires that you learn certain fundamentals before you can effectively play the game. The basics include the proper mental attitude, a variety of practice and reading hand motions, practice drills, and various strategies for better concentration, comprehension, and recall.

The proper attitude to learn speed reading requires that you set specific, realistic long-term and short-term goals, act as if your goals have already been accomplished, and then let no one discourage you. State or write your goals (left brain) and visualize the end result clearly and vividly (right brain) while in a relaxed state.

Practicing is going at a rate of speed faster than you can understand. The purpose of practicing is to increase reading speed. Practice drills adjust your eyes and mind to progressively faster rates. A secondary purpose of practicing is to perfect the mechanics of speed reading. The physical elements of speed reading include eye/hand coordination, an open focus, smooth, rhythmic hand motions, and page turning. The mental aspects of speed reading include the Slash Memory Tree, book control, and visualization.

The mental part of the game of speed reading starts with concentration. To improve your ability to concentrate, you must integrate all the elements in the *AAIRR* formula: attitude, attention, interest, relaxation, and repetition. To concentrate while speed reading, flood your mind with positive words, pictures, and emotions while you are in a relaxed state. Then set specific and realistic goals while reducing as many internal and external distractions as is possible. Interest is the fuel for concentration. If you lack interest, replace interest with other motivating factors. Finally, repetition is necessary to allow certain basics of speed reading to become subconscious, so that more of your mind's energy focuses on your reading purpose as opposed to the mechanics.

Good concentration is an element of good comprehension, but it's not the only one. To achieve your best comprehension, you must also eliminate learning barriers, acquire a solid knowledge base, and have a specific purpose or strong need.

There are a number of important psychological factors that affect your memory when you read or study. First, you are more likely to remember items that fall at the beginning and end of a particular sequence and more likely to forget what falls in the middle. Second, memory declines quickly after learning, but an immediate review of the material can save much of the information from being forgotten. Third, memory improves if you divide large learning assignments into equal parts of no more than forty minutes and then separate them by short breaks. Fourth, a brief review of information learned previously will improve memory when learning new information. Fifth, in lists of similar items we are more likely to recall unusual or outstanding items. Sixth, the capacity of short-term, left brain memory is seven units plus or minus two; however, if you increase the size of each unit, you can recall much more information. Seventh, your right brain memory has no such limitations and can recall an infinite number of pictures or images.

Two main factors that affect your memory are the principles of association and organization. Association is a connecting or triggering process. Everything you have stored in your brain acts as hooks to learn new information. Organization allows you to file and retrieve information from your mind. A mnemonic-organized base combines association and organization to form powerful memory systems such as the Alphabet and Room Systems.

The RWAP study system stands for Repetition With A Purpose. The basis of the system is that you must repeat detailed or difficult reading more than once. Each repetition has a distinct purpose as you move from general to specific information until you satisfy your reading purpose. The basic system is as follows:

1. Overview the material to become familiar with the book's structure.
2. Determine your purpose.
3. Do a general pre-read to locate main ideas for the entire reading.
4. Divide the reading into manageable sections. For each section do the following:
  a. Specific pre-read for main ideas only.
  b. Read for details.
  c. Summarize in your own words.
  d. Take a short break (five to ten minutes).
  e. Repeat until the assignment is completed.
5. Post-read at the end of the entire reading from back to front as a final check before moving on.
6. Review at spaced intervals.

Taking notes with the Slash Memory Tree has a number of advantages over the conventional outline form in improving your understanding and retention of reading or lecture material. The Slash Memory Tree brings both sides of your brain into the note-taking process by making a verbal and visual representation of the material. The Memory Tree's format has you organize the information as you write it down. Furthermore, the Slash Memory Tree is fun, unusual, and extremely flexible.

You now have all the ingredients in place to make you the best reader possible—all except one. The last element is practice and without it, all the others are for naught. Practice will allow your eyes and hand to move together naturally. You'll establish a purpose and visualize without having to give the process any conscious thought, and the concentration and memory techniques will become part of you. The next six weeks are the most crucial. Continue to play the game of speed reading on a daily basis. Relax, have fun, and transform speed reading into a lifelong skill and learning into a lifelong goal.

DAILY PROGRESS REPORT SHEET

Date	Practice Rate	Reading Rate	Est. Comp. %	Time Practiced

DAILY PROGRESS REPORT SHEET

Date	Practice Rate	Reading Rate	Est. Comp. %	Time Practiced

DAILY PROGRESS REPORT SHEET

Date	Practice Rate	Reading Rate	Est. Comp. %	Time Practiced

DAILY PROGRESS REPORT SHEET

Date	Practice Rate	Reading Rate	Est. Comp. %	Time Practiced

DAILY PROGRESS REPORT SHEET

Date	Practice Rate	Reading Rate	Est. Comp. %	Time Practiced

DAILY PROGRESS REPORT SHEET

Date	Practice Rate	Reading Rate	Est. Comp. %	Time Practiced

DAILY PROGRESS REPORT SHEET

Date	Practice Rate	Reading Rate	Est. Comp. %	Time Practiced

INDEX